# THE LADY FROM STALINGRAD MANSIONS

This is the latest in a long line of hilarious books by
Alan Coren which includes the highly successful
IDI AMIN books, THE DOG IT WAS THAT DIED and
THE SANITY INSPECTOR. The author, who has a
large and enthusiastic following on both sides of the
Atlantic, is editor of *Punch*, television critic for *The
Times* and weekly columnist for the *Evening Standard*
and he broadcasts regularly on radio and television.

'He writes with a kind of divine spark.'
*Daily Telegraph*

'Mr. Coren is that rare thing – a genuinely funny writer.'
*Daily Mirror*

'One of the funniest writers I have ever read from any
country.'
*Esquire*

'Constantly funny, constantly true.'
*Evening Standard*

# The Lady from Stalingrad Mansions

## Alan Coren

CORONET BOOKS
Hodder and Stoughton

The author would like to thank the proprietors of PUNCH magazine for permission to reproduce material in this book.

First published in Great Britain 1977
by Robson Books Limited

British Library C.I.P.
Coren, Alan
   The Lady from Stalingrad Mansions.
   I. Title
   828'.9'1408                    PN6175
   ISBN  0–340–23095–9

*Coronet edition 1978*

Printed and bound in Great Britain for Hodder and Stoughton Paperbacks, a division of Hodder and Stoughton Ltd., Mill Road, Dunton Green, Sevenoaks, Kent (Editorial Office: 47 Bedford Square, London, WC1 3DP) by Richard Clay (The Chaucer Press) Ltd., Bungay, Suffolk

# CONTENTS

# Prolegomenon

You don't find many prolegomena around these days.

Forewords, yes; introductions, certainly; prefaces, by the gross. But when was the last time you saw a book with a prolegomenon from even that most prolific of literary comperes, HRH? And if you can't get a prolegomenon from a Greek, for heaven's sake, where *can* you get it?

It may well be the fault of the publishers, of course. Time was, an English publisher was a loose pile of uncoordinated lovat tweed, lightly dusted with snuff, among which a monocle might be seen glinting, not unlike an amoeba's nucleus. His main function was to poke the fires in large Bloomsbury offices, pour brown sherry into writers, point out paternally that sentences were things which you mustn't put a preposition on the end of, and retail Macedonian anecdotes dropped by Gilbert Murray, in flawless Wykehamist Greek.

Not any longer. The modern publisher doubtless thinks prolegomenon is a new up-market board game of which he has not yet, by some oversight on his secretary's part, heard; and will, upon hearing the word now, immediately rush round to Asprey's and attempt to order it in a monogrammed crocodile box with 22-carat fittings. For they are men of the media now, and much given to thinking of words as products sold in an oblong box which opens at the side.

Fortunately, though, it is still possible for an author to steal a march on them. An author, to pluck an example at random from the hypothetical air, may find a yellow flimsy in the post saying: WHY BOOK CALLED LADY FROM STALINGRAD MANSIONS? But by the time the author has picked up the phone to explain, the publisher is strapped aboard an eastbound Concorde in a supersonic bid to flog the Bahreini rights.

Leaving his desk unattended.

So that the author can slip in quietly and leave a prolegomenon on it; which, such is the speed at which the modern computerized publishing industry works, will be down at the printers and bound into the finished book while the publisher is still doubled up over his first sheep's eye.

The result being that the publisher is just as surprised as anyone else to discover, on publication day, that the product is called *The Lady from Stalingrad Mansions* for no other reason than that the author rather likes the title.

Well, one other reason; but a very small one. Because the lady from Stalingrad Mansions does appear in the text, just once, and very fleetingly. You have to read every single word to find her.

Call it author's revenge.

*Bare Essentials*

**London Edition**

London - Paris - Rome - New York -Hollywood

THE
## CELEBRITY BULLETIN
10, Dover Street, London, WIX 3PH

499 8511

WEEK  F TUESDAY, 28th SEPTEMBER
- MONDAY 4th  CTOBER, 1976

WHAT THEY ARE DOING THIS WEEK:          HERE.

| | |
|---|---|
| MICHAEL PENNINGTON and<br>CHERIE LUNGHI | will open on Tuesday in "DESTINY" at The<br>Other Place, Stratford-upon-Avon. |
| ALAN COREN and<br>EUGENE IONESCO | will open at the Phoenix Theatre on<br>Thursday, in "CARTE BLANCHE". |
| STAN KENTON and | will appear in concert at the Fairfield |

Established 1952

IF YOU RING the number listed above, and if you ask how it comes about that Alan Coren and Eugene Ionesco should be appearing in Mr Tynan's latest flesh-mortifying erotorama, a very nice lady will—as far as it is possible to do so over the telephone—blush, and tell you that it is all a terrible mistake for which they have already apologised to an incensed Mr Coren, whose relatives have been jumping out of high windows rather than face the opprobrium attendant upon the scion of their ancient line running round in public with his clothes off.

Yet despite her fulsomely apologetic denials, may there not still be some unkind souls out there who, when they see smoke, shout 'Fire!'? Is it not possible, I hear some of you say, that literati eke out their paltry livings by leading such devious double lives?

Should I, in short, come clean?

How strange that history is almost invariably made in inauspicious places! To think that the revolution which was to change not just the theatre but the whole tone and temper of modern convention should have undergone its birth pangs at that lowly environ, the Alhambra, Bradford!

We had been engaged to open the second half on that chill February Monday, just a few short years ago: IONESCO & AL, A JOKE, A SONG, A SMILE. We were in our bleak little bedsitter in Mrs Compton-Burnett's Theatrical Boarding House, wiring our revolving bow-ties to the batteries in our hats and polishing the climax of our act (*Ionesco: 'My dog's got no nose.' Me: 'Your dog's got no nose? How does he smell?' Ionesco: 'Awful!'*) when there was the most fearful thumping and barking from the floor above.

'Stone me!' cried Ionesco, snatching off his rubber conk in

justifiable irritation. 'How do they expect us to rehearse with all that bleeding racket going on? Are we artistes or are we not?' He hopped to the door on his giant shoes, and wrenched it open. 'IVY!' he roared.

Mrs Compton-Burnett came heavily up the creaking stairs. She pushed a wisp of ginger hair under her mob-cap with a dripping soup-ladle.

'Madame,' said Ionesco, hand on hip, left profile tilted to the bulblight, 'us acolytes of bleeding Thespis are at pains to . . .'

'It's T. S. Eliot,' said Mrs Compton-Burnett, 'he's got that bloody seal upstairs with him again. I don't know how many times I've told him.' She leaned into the stairwell. 'YOU BRING 'IM DOWN OUT OF THERE, MR ELIOT!' she shrieked. 'I GOT ENOUGH TROUBLE WITHOUT CODS' HEADS IN THE S-BEND!'

An upstairs door opened, and T. S. Eliot's top-hatted head appeared over the banister.

'Boris is an artiste,' he shouted. 'You cannot expect him to spend his days juggling jam-jars on his hooter and his nights in a bloody toolshed! A seal has his pride, too.'

'Well, some of us is trying to synchronise revolving bows and funny walks down here,' Ionesco shouted back. 'Don't bloody mind us, mate!'

'TENANTS OF THE HOUSE!' yelled Eliot. 'THOUGHTS OF A DRY BRAIN IN A DRY SEASON!'

He slammed the door again.

'Patter!' snapped Ionesco. 'That's all he is, bloody patter. First house Monday night at Bradford, who gives a toss whether he should have been a pair of ragged claws scuttling across the floors of silent seas? Get the seal on, get your plates up on your sticks, tell 'em the one about the one-legged undertaker, and get off. Never mind your bleeding patter!'

The door across the landing opened, and two fat men in fright wigs emerged. Between them stood a balding midget.

'I don't think you've met Evelyn Waugh's Harmonica Fools,' said Mrs Compton-Burnett. 'Evelyn, Alec, and little Auberon.'

We all shook hands.

'Only trying to rehearse the bloody *Thunder And Lightning Polka*, weren't we?' said Evelyn, testily. 'Got into the middle twelve and going like the bloody clappers, suddenly there's all this shouting, Morris the Musical Dog bites Alec in the leg, little Auberon falls off his shoulders, bang!'

Mrs Compton-Burnett stroked the midget's pate.

'Did he hurt himself, then?' she murmured.

The midget opened its mouth, and a strange discordant wheeze came out.

'Only swallowed his wossname, hasn't he?' snapped Evelyn. 'His organ.'

'What will you do?' I said.

'I'll have a heart attack, that's what I'll do,' said Evelyn. 'I'll bang my head on the wall. Better ideas you got?'

'We should never have left Poland,' said Alec.

They went back inside.

'Come on,' said Ionesco, 'we're on in half an hour, and J. B. Priestley's borrowed my bloody monocycle, we'll have to take the short cut across the allotments.'

A far door opened.

'*Across the allotments?*' cried a voice. 'Why, as you wend your way 'twixt elm and privet, who is this bounding up to you? "Arf, arf!" it goes. "Why, it is Rover the dog!" you cry, "and who is this with him?" "Baa, baa!" "Goodness me!" you exclaim, taken somewhat aback, "what is this little lamb doing so near the pig-sty?" "Oink, oink!" the pigs inform us, their little . . .'

We went back to our own room, and shut the door.

'C. P. Snow,' explained Ionesco. 'A professional to his finger-tips. Ever heard his starling?'

I shook my head.

'A masterpiece,' said Ionesco. 'I seen him do it riding bareback at Bertram Mills' one Christmas, I'll never forget it. 'Course, I'm going back a bit now. It was when he was with Compton Mackenzie's Elephant Ensemble.'

'They were great days, I understand,' I said.

'The best, son,' said Ionesco, his eyes moistening. 'Remember Graham Greene & His Krazy Kar? That was one of the Queen Mother's favourites, you know. She used to send Graham a pound of cobnuts from the Sandringham estates every Guy Fawkes' Night. We go back a long way, him and me. I knew him when he was Brian Breene.'

'I didn't know he'd changed his name,' I said.

'Had to,' said Ionesco. 'Started out as a ventriloquist. The dummy used to introduce him, and afterwards people'd come up to him in the street and say "I know you, you're Grian Greene" so he decided to make life easier for himself.'

We packed our props and stage suits in our hold-alls, went downstairs through the reek of cabbage and dove-droppings, and walked briskly through the sleet to the theatre.

Stone-faced matrons thronged the foyer, and bronchitic British Legionnaires, and drunks with Brasso bottles in their hip-pockets, and malevolent small boys a-gleam with bright acne. There was a smell of rainsoaked dandruff.

'Bloody hell!' said Ionesco, the seams lengthening in his sad Rumanian face. 'I'd rather be opening the first half, son, before they've had a chance to get their eye in. It'll be like the bloody Somme after the interval.'

We crept past them, and down the back stairs to the mean little dressing-room we shared with Angus Wilson. He was sitting slumped in the corner, in his horse's head. There was despair written all over the little white legs poking out beneath the dappled torso.

'What's up, then, Angus?' said Ionesco.

The head turned, very slowly, towards us. Its glass eyes rolled.

'Me hindquarters,' it said, 'have gone down with sciatica. I just heard.'

'No!' cried Ionesco, 'old Betjeman not turned up?'

'Crippled,' muttered the horse. 'Lying there like Gregor bleeding Samsa. What am I going to do?'

'*We're* not on till the second half!' I cried, in true showbiz tradition. 'Why don't I do the back legs for you? It's the easy bit, no singing or juggling involved, just the tap-dance at the end.'

'It's very nice of him, Eugene,' said the horse, 'but he doesn't understand, does he?'

'You don't understand,' said Ionesco, to me. 'Angus can't get in a horse with any Tom, Dick or Harry, no offence meant. It's a very intimate relationship. It's got to be built up over the wossname, years.'

'It wouldn't feel right,' said the horse.

'Look,' said Ionesco. 'Suppose we both got in?'

'Don't talk bloody daft,' said the horse. 'Six legs hanging down? We'd look like a giant ant. I'm not billed as ANGUS THE WONDER INSECT, am I?'

'I didn't mean that,' said Ionesco. 'You go off home, me and him'll do your act. The management'll never know.'

'Would you really?' cried the horse.

'Say no more!' replied Ionesco.

We went on fourth, after H. E. BATES, WIZARD OF THE XYLOPHONE, and we managed well enough, despite some personal embarrassment during the somersault, but when we returned to our dressing-room, we found ourselves to be so sweat-wrung that there was nothing for it but to take off the underwear in which we had performed the act and hang it in front of the electric fire to dry. After which we turned to our mirrors in order to make up for our own act. So intent was I upon this, that I did not notice the smell until Ionesco suddenly turned from his dressing-table and said:

'What's burning?'

'Burning?' I said, 'I don't . . .'

'FIRE!' shrieked Ionesco, and I looked round, and our underwear had not only ignited, but had also set fire to the curtains! As the flames licked the pelmets, Ionesco and I rushed, naked, for the door.

The corridor was packed. C. P. Snow was mooing expertly to himself, The Singing Pakenhams were combing one another's coifs, Cyril Connolly and Doris were shoving cards up one another's sleeves—the exit was completely blocked!

'Come on!' cried Ionesco, and we took off in the opposite direction, not knowing, in our panic, where we were going, until, suddenly, we burst through a door and found ourselves in the middle of the spotlit stage, from which the previous act (W. H. AUDEN, HE FILLS THE STAGE WITH FLAGS) had just made his exit.

The audience roared!

The audience shrieked!

The audience cheered!

'Come on!' I hissed, grabbing his bare arm. 'Let's get off!'

'*Get off?*' cried Ionesco. 'GET OFF? Laddie, we'll never get a reception like this again!' He threw an arm around my naked shoulder. 'I say, I say, I say!' he shouted. 'What's got nine legs, three ears, and walks like my Uncle Bert?'

It was still not too late for me to run, but the applause of the crowd filled my ears, and the smell of the greasepaint, and the blaze of the lights, and all those wonderful things ravished my senses, and . . .

'I don't know,' I replied, 'what *has* got nine . . .'

And after that, we never looked back.

# And This Is The Little Appliance

*'Despite the new Sex Equality laws, most British males will continue to treat their wives as more or less useful objects'* – Time *magazine*

'COME HOME FRIDAY, didn't I?' said the man in the blue dungarees, fingernailing a speck of nut from his beer-froth, 'and what was there? Pile of washing on the kitchen floor, dinner with the frost still on it, cat's doings in the corner by the telly. I thought, Gawd bleeding blind O'Reilly, it's packed up again!'

'And had it?' enquired the man in the herringbone overcoat, over the rim of his glass.

'Completely,' said the man in the blue dungarees. 'There it was in the corner. I gave it a poke, it just sort of wobbled a bit.'

'You can try kicking 'em,' said the man in the Wimpey jacket. 'It sometimes gets 'em going. Especially on cold mornings.'

The man in the dungarees finished his pint, and sucked the froth from his moustache.

'No,' he said, 'I could tell this was a skilled job. You don't want to go mucking about with 'em when it might be something radical. You could do a hell of a lot of damage. I gave mine a shake a couple of years back, turned out it had dislocated itself going after cobwebs. I put its bloody shoulder out. I didn't get it back for a fortnight. You wouldn't believe the state of my hosiery, time it got started again.'

'So what did you do this time?' asked the man in the herringbone overcoat, returning from the bar with three fresh pints.

The man in the blue dungarees drank a third off, belched, shrugged.

'Had to phone up, didn't I, get a man in. Not easy. He

wanted me to bring it to him, first off. All that way, must be two miles, dragging that great big thing.'

'You could give yourself a rupture,' said the man in the herringbone overcoat.'You could rip a sleeve, dragging.'

'That's what I told him. He come round, finally. Well past dinner-time, I might say. I had to get a pork pie down the wossname, the pub. Anyway, he had a look at it, had a feel underneath, shone his light in, listened with his stethoscope.'

'What was wrong?'

'Varicose veins,' said the man in the blue dungarees. 'Can you credit it?'

The other two looked at him, shocked.

*'Varicose veins?'* said the man in the herringbone overcoat. 'I can't see why that stops 'em cooking. You don't bloody cook with your legs, or am I mistaken?'

'I had the veins go on mine, once,' said the man in the Wimpey jacket. 'I put it right myself. What you do is, you bind the legs up with elastic bandage. Get it anywhere, Boots, anywhere. Did the whole lot for under a quid.'

'I'm not handy that way,' said the man in the blue dungarees. 'I'd probably make a muck of it. Stop its circulation, or sunnink. Legs'd probably fall off, and then where would I be? Eating out of tins, getting a laundry to deliver, it could cost a fortune. Anyway, he said the veins were affecting it all over, it'd have to go away and have 'em done proper.'

'Bloody hell,' said the man in the herringbone overcoat, 'how long will that take?'

The man in the blue dungarees pursed his lips.

'He couldn't say right off,' he said. 'They got work piled up to here, apparently. Might not be able to fit mine in for six months. And once they've got it up on the bench, it could take a fortnight to get it going proper. And *then,*' he added bitterly, 'you got to run 'em in for a bit. Light work only, no standing, no lifting.'

'The state your floors'll be in!' said the man in the Wimpey jacket. 'It don't bear thinking about. Not to mention the other.'

'The other?'

'The ironing. It's got to stand up to iron. I got mine ironing once in the non-standing position when it got water on its knees, you ought to have seen the state of my blue worsted, it had flat sleeves and three bleeding lapels.'

'I know,' said the man in the blue dungarees morosely. 'I said to the bloke, bloody hell, I said, it's only forty-three, you don't expect 'em to start going at forty-three, it ought to have thirty years left in it before a major wossname, overhaul. Rate it's going on, I said, it'll start needing new bits before long. I might have to put a lung in it, or something, and Gawd knows what that could cost.'

The man in the herringbone overcoat shook his head.

'Can't put lungs in,' he said. 'They can get along on one lung—mind you, it slows 'em down getting upstairs with tea, you'll have to reckon on putting the alarm on a good quarter of an hour earlier—but if they both pack up, that's it.'

'I never realised,' said the man in the blue dungarees. 'You see where they put new hearts in and everything, I thought you could just go on replacing with spares.'

'You want to watch yours,' said the man in the Wimpey jacket. 'I hope I'm not speaking out of turn, but I saw it once, cleaning out the coalhouse in the rain. It can ruin 'em, leaving 'em out in the rain. *And* it was smoking. Combination of rain and smoking, them lungs it's got won't be fit for blowing on your porridge in a year or two.'

The man in the herringbone overcoat nodded.

'You ought to look after it better,' he said. 'It pays off in the end. Stop it smoking, for a start. And if it's got to go out in the rain, you ought to get one of them plastic hoods to tie over it. You can get 'em at Woolies. Five bob, but it's worth it. My old man looked after his a treat, he was a bit of a fanatic really, he used to keep it spotless. Once the dirt gets in the wrinkles, he used to say, they start to go. Do you know, when he popped his clogs, it was still going like the clappers, after nearly eighty years. Someone said I ought to give it to an old folks' home; bugger that, I said, that's got a lot left in it, that has, so I installed it in the attic. It was still doing little jobs, making sandwiches, sewing, till it was nearly ninety. Released mine for all sorts of major work. That's how I got the extension built.'

The man in the blue dungarees sighed.

'They don't make 'em like that no more,' he said. 'Mine had to have glasses before it was thirty. It was either that or put forty-watt bulbs in, and you know how they burn it. It's going to need a deaf aid soon, as well, I'm sick of shouting for the evening paper now it can't hear the whistle over the noise of the egg-whisk. That's four batteries a year, for a start, not to mention initial outlay.'

'British,' said the man in the Wimpey jacket, 'that's the trouble.'

'What?'

'British. Load of bleeding tat. If I had my time over again, I'd get a Jap one. They're beautifully put together. Brother had a Jap, got it out east thirty years ago, it still ties his shoe-laces of a morning.'

'No!'

'Gerroff!'

'Straight up,' said the man in the Wimpey jacket. 'Also makes furniture out of old newspaper. Not to mention bloody accurate. Send it down the shops, it never gets short-changed, never buys the wrong thing, never comes back two minutes late on account of not assessing bus connections efficiently. It's saved him a packet, over the years.'

The man in the blue dungarees leaned forward, slightly uneasily.

'Tell me,' he said, 'this Jap. Does it get, er, headaches?'

'At night, he means,' said the man in the herringbone overcoat.

'I know what he bloody means!' snapped the man in the Wimpey jacket. 'I got a British one, haven't I? No,' he said to the man in the blue dungarees, 'as I understand it, it has never had a headache in its life. Night after night after night, my brother says, it don't suffer from headaches.'

The three of them sat in silence after this, for some time.

'Funny thing about British models,' said the man in the blue dungarees, at last. 'You can't help feeling they got a basic design flaw in 'em somewhere.'

'That's what it is, all right,' said the man in the Wimpey jacket.

# French Leave

*October 26 having been designated Au Pair Day, I couldn't help wondering how the average girl would spend it.*

SUNDAY, OCTOBER 26

Allo, mah diary! Nem of a dog, but wot a day ah em avving! Ow lucky ah em zat tomorro eez mah day off and Tuesday eez mah arf day and Wednesday eez mah free morning, uzzerwise ah wood nevair be fit for mah rest day on Sursday weech ah nid to, ow you say, set mi up for zer wikkend.

Bicause today eez National Au Pair Day, Mistair Griswole bring mi up breakfuss in bed. Normally, eet eez Missus Griswole oo bring eet up, but hi explane where today eez a special occasion, also Missus Griswole feelin very weery wot weeth zer ousework zer cheeldren zer washin zer ironin zer shoppin, on top of havin to shorten mah frok for Au Pair Day an clin mah bes shoes good.

Aftair brekfuss, ah tek a nise ot barf until aroun arf past ten, but holy blue! Imagin mah surprise wen ah open zer barfroom dor aftairwards an oo shuld fall on mi but Mistair Griswole oo ave fall aslip leenin on zer dor! Hi eez very apologisin, but ah cri: 'Zink nussin of eet, Mistair Griswole, you can grab mah ches anytime, ha-ha-ha!' This mek Mistair Griswole go orible wite an weespair: 'For God's sake kip your voise down, Nicole, ah weel len you car, ah weel by you beeg botl of Chanel!'

Poor Mistair Groswole! Hi nid to tek barf bicause hi covaired in blak dus from bringin in cole (wich eez normly Missus Griswole's job), but hi fine no ot watair no more, so he spen nex arf our running up an down stairs wiz ketls.

Eet is amazin ow hi kip his tempair, wot wiz zer cheeldren scrimmin for their breakfuss an zer dog owlin to bi let out an Missus Griswole obblin about lookin for her migrane pils an zer telephone ringin all zer time. Ah sink ah weel ave to ave mah own phone put in: zer calls are always for mi, an eet eez a terrible waste of time for zer Griswoles to kip runnin up to mah room wiz messages wen they bofe ave so much to do aroun zer ouse.

Mine you, mah diary, ah wonder sometimes eef they do not tek advantage. Only yesterday, wen she was polishin mah dressin-table, Missus Griswole ask me eef ah em available for baby-sittin on December 19. 'Missus Griswole!' ah exclem. 'Ow on erse can ah know wot ah weel be doin two ole munce from now?'

Enyway, at eleven o'clock zis mornin, ah set off to meet wiz mah frens to celebrate Au Pair Day: first, wi are to attend a church in Ampstead Garden Suburb where special prayers are offaired to zer Blessed Françoise, Patron Saint of Au Pairs, who drop ded in 1574 wen someone ask her to scrub a flor. Wi are all there, but Ilse mah bes frend eez a litle late bicause her employer, Mistair Dickinson, ave back his car into zer wall wen gettin eet out to give her a lift, an Ilse ave to ang about for ages while Mistair Dickinson run to zer top of zer road to fine a taxi.

Aftair church, Ilse's boy fren come by in his car to drive us up to town. Lefty eez a nise boy, excep he only ave one eer an his noze eez flat; he eez very genrous, an evry time me or Ilse or any of our frens tell im anything, such as wen our employers are goin off on ollyday or oo kip zer key on a string inside zer letter-box or wich florboard you ave to lift up to find zer coco tin wiz zer diamonds in it, Lefty always give er sumsing good for erself, like a candelabra or a nise bag of led. Eet eez a bit crowded in Lefty's car, tho, bicause he already ave three Spanish au pairs in zer back wich he eez deliverin to customers of his escort service. Zer girls are all shiverin a bit, wot wiz wearin only fishnet stockins an raincoats, but Lefty soon cheer them up tellin them about how he settin up zis feelm wiz Robert Redford nex Friday an all of them goin to be big stars.

Well, mah diary, Lefty drop Ilse an me off in Arley Strit where zer Portland Clinique is givin a beeg celebration lunch in honneur of Au Pair Day, jus as a way of saying Sank You to all customers ole an new, includin all our frens in zer cab trade, an mah secon-best fren Gracia turn out to be zer gest of honneur. She mek a spich in wich she say zat wizzout zer Portland an eets wonderful staff, she would now be a muzzer of fourteen, an ze thought mek her go deezy bicause everybody know ow difficult eet eez to get staff these days!

Evryone larf very loud at zis. Gracia eez a one, an no mistek! Ah fil sure she could ave a marvellous career on zer stage, eef only she did not ave her art set on marryin into zer rag trade. Las year she come very close to pullin eet off wiz a very nise guy oo ave a Lamborghini Espada an a yacht an eez a director of eighteen blouse companies, only his father fine out about eet an say zer guy eez too yung to marry at fourteen, an punch his hed.

Aftair lunch, mah diary, we pay a viseet to zer Home Office Au Pair Exhibition in Whitehall where we lissen to a very interestin lecture from a lawyer who explen ow we mus not let ourselves be exploits, an zen we look at all zer exhibits like zer new 45-inch colour TV etcetera, but ah do not sink ah weel ask zer Griswoles for one bicause eet do not ave a remote control attachment an ah do not weesh to be jumpin out of my barf all zer time to change channels. Personally, ah prefair zis new pushchair wiz zer 125cc moteur, eet tek al zer effort out of shoppin wiz zer cheeldren an Missus Griswole weel ave energy lef to cook an ot lunch wen she get ome. Ah do not mine smoke sammon an cole duk, but not evry day. Ilse say she most impressed wiz zer new range of baby-bouncers wich ave been specialy strengthened to tek all cheeldren up to zer age of seexteen. As her employer ave five, Ilse weel be able to string zem all up after breakfuss and leave zem danglin wile she get on wiz her correspondence.

By zer time we come out of zer exhibition, eet eez gettin dark, an Ilse suggest we see one of zer feelms zat zer Soho Sexima eez puttin on in honneur of zer occasion. Eet turn out to be *Swidish Au Pair Nude Leather Wikkend A-Go-Go;* eet eez quite interestin, but for me eet eez spoil by zer prepostrous fantasie: at zer start of zer feelm, we see Ingrid dustin an polishin! Ah ave a good mine to write to mah Ambassadeur an complain: zis kine of feelm weel put bad ideas into people's heds.

Aftair zer feelm, we fine ourselves at a loose end: shall we go to zer Eurofunky Disco An Engleesh Language Collidge in Regent Strit? Aftair all, Mistair Griswole ave already pay zer ninety pound for zis term wich include entry fee to all social functions, but wen ah suggest to Ilse zat we drop in for a smoke, she tel me zat zer collidge ave bin busted las wik on account of zer Eadmaster ave bin caught in possession, also police lookin into zer fac zat Missus Ogalidogliou, zer Matron, ave not return from Beirut wiz her party of twelve Norwegian girls.

'Wot about zer Manila Nitespot?' suggest Ilse, but ah tel her ah cannot stand zis place bicause zer Filipinos always go aroun in couples an knife anyone oo look like they could be competition for a nise self-contain flat over the garage.

So we end up back at Gracia's ouse in Souse Kensington. She ave chuck out her employers for zer wikkend an lock zer kids in zer cellar an call up Fortnum an Mason to wizz roun a few dozen lobstaire an pâté de foie gras an so on, an wot weeth her boy frens knowin ow to jemmy open a cocktail cabinet, evrybody avin a wonairful time an not realisin ow late it get until zer Fire Brigade turn up an complen about bein call out at four a.m. jus to put out a blazin Picasso, an why could not someone simply chuck a bucket of watair over it, but Gracia explainin zat she do not know where zer buckets are kept, so it turns out all right aftair all.

Mine you, mah diary, Mistair Griswole eez also a beet put out to be call at arf past five to tek me ome, but wen ah point out zat ah em jus a simple country girl oo eez afraid of wanderin about zer beeg city alone, ah sink he understand.

# I'll Have A Rubber Bone, Thanks Very Much, And The Wife Would Like A Large Worm Powder

THIS BEING that time of year when the paterfamilial skull begins to hum and the entrail to knot at the imminence of that annual *schweinfest* during which normal happy families are snatched from their normal happy homes and dumped down in far alien spots, there to be ravaged, at considerable expense, by gastro-enteritis, tar, sunstroke, carnivorous plumbing, insults, daylight robbery, rude service, noise, crabs in the shoe, and a wonderful local wine make from old torch batteries, I thought it no bad moment to direct everyone's jaded attention to the sort of holiday of which most of us can only dream.

This is because most of us have two legs and, for all the good it's done us, discourse of reason.

You have, of course, guessed by now that my text this week is taken from *Pets Welcome!*, subtitled *The Animal Lovers' Holiday Guide*, an engaging little volume which runs out at only 50p, including a full-colour front cover which shows one of the crack editorial team, the nubile Miss Christine Richards, fondling, on an empty beach, Mr Twink (a marmalade cat), and a full-colour back cover which offers *The Glaxo Guide To Heat In Bitches;* which only goes to show how magazine design can run away from you if you take your mind off it for even a split second.

The first half of this helpful book is low-keyed enough, content merely to list those hotels and boarding houses which actually welcome pets, an invaluable catalogue for holiday-makers who might otherwise turn up at the Hotel Spendide, Frinton, only to have their emu set upon by bouncers and their entire vacation written off. But it is in the second half that the dreams are dreamed, and the promises held out which human brochures would not dare to frame; it is in the second half where you and I are made to regret that our ancestors decided, on a whim, to try rising from the crouch. The second half is about animal hotels.

Take the Pussytel and Boarding Kennels, Clophill: *Each pet has its own private villa with its own personal run; infra-red heating; lovely country surrounding; licensed,* and, still in Clophill (which must be a sort of feline Antibes), The Sealawn Boarding Cattery: *Cats; accommodation in cabins or penthouses, thermally insulated; large exercise run with ladders and sunning shelves, licensed; great attention to hygiene; pleasant garden setting in 3½ acres of grounds.*

Dear God, to be a cat in Clophill this July! With great attention to one's hygiene paid (do lissome chambermaids come in and lick you, giggling the while?); lolling alone in one's private villa or penthouse safe from screaming kids requiring a victim for beach burial; sunning oneself on an individual shelf, sleeping off whatever it is cats knock back on these licensed premises; with a ladder to run up, should the urge to exercise arise.

Nothing about all-night discotheques detonating *Volare* under your window, or mandatory, hundred-strong bus excursions to bullfights and glassblowings, nothing about packed swimming-pools opaque with Ambre Solaire and even nastier decantings, nothing about boutiques with brass castanets that play *The Bluebells Of Scotland* and fall to bits when unwrapped, nothing about having your laundry personally shredded by madmen.

You just sleep in the sun, get washed, get fed, run up your ladder, sleep in the sun, get drunk, run up your ladder, sleep in the . . .

There are, however, one or two drawbacks in Clophill which should be pointed out, at least at Pussytel: *Entire toms,* it says, *not accepted.* It is a discreet little note, and I would guess that it does not refer to guests short of an eye, say, as the result of some valiant nocturnal brawl, or missing a hind leg. I think it means that they run a clean joint at Pussytel, and do not wish any intercourse between the private villas after the sun goes down, and certainly this is one minus when we set the place against its human equivalent. There is a limit to the sacrifices one is prepared to make for lovely country surroundings.

Still, you'd be all right at Sealawn. Nothing worse is required there than statutory inoculation against feline enteritis, and that's probably no worse than a bad cold.

They're even freer-thinking down in Steeple Aston, mind, where the Elmsgate kennels go out of their way to sympathise with the drives that lie behind some customers' annual fortnights away from it all: *Large dog runs; licensed; bitches in season welcomed* runs their refreshingly straightforward rubric (compare it with the nudgy innuendo about 'Singles' you find in the average travel agent's bumf), but before the more liberated pets start chucking their things into a holdall, they might do well to read on. It may not be a swinger's paradise, after all. For a line later we find *Un-neutered toms not accepted*. Personally, I cannot but believe that this arrangement will lead to friction; it cannot be easy for a neutered tom, lying on his shelf and trying to get a bit of kip while animals not only spared the knife but also in their seasonal prime rattle the floorboards of the penthouse upstairs, tearing up and down their ladders and generally enjoying the sort of holiday that normally only goes with the Presidency of the United States.

Nevertheless, there is still no reason why the Elmsgate guests should not have the holidays of their lives, and holidays immeasurably more delightful than their masters', provided that a modicum of soundproofing is provided and a few stout fences, as I'm sure is the case. It would certainly have to be the case chez Mrs E. A. Webster, Rosemead, Pynest Green Lane, Waltham Abbey: *Dogs (60), Cats (48), also Caged Birds, Rabbits, Tortoises, etcetera* (etcetera?); at Meadowbank Pets Holiday Home, Lymington: *Cats, Tortoises, Hamsters, Caged Birds, Goldfish;* and at Northfield Boarding Kennels, near Royston, who are willing, dear heaven, to do package deals on: *Dogs (60), Cats (5), Budgies, Parrots, Rabbits, Guinea Pigs, Mice, etcetera* (I wish I hadn't squandered that ? just now; how much more etcetera can you get than holidaymaking mice?).

And there, at these remarkably ambitious leisure centres, free from all the pressures that beset you and me upon our fraught Costas, the little furry friends gambol and disport, running up ladders—or, in the case of tortoises, staring up ladders—pinging their bells, whizzing round their individuated aquaria wolfing ants' eggs on the half-shell, while the parrots call one another Charlie and swop raunchy stories of Dorking boudoirs, and the mice do whatever it is mice do on their fortnight off.

Yes, friends, a holiday idyll, an annual ark, a recurring Disney documentary of harmony and *gemütlichkeit* beneath the infra-red heating and overlooking the fetching acreage of English greensward.

Or is it?

Is this just another holiday fantasy like all the rest? Do the animals in fact turn up at their selected funspots expecting the brochure made life, only to find that it is only ordinary life, after all? Does the penthouse turn out to be too small to swing a cat, or rather mouse, in? Does the shelf fall off as you spring on it for a bit of sun, does the heating go off when it's cold and come on when it's hot, does the un-neutered tom next door turn out to have everything intact and constantly grab you while you're waiting in line for your codsheads, do, conversely, the bitches on heat turn out to be elderly matrons with wall-eyes who spend all day swopping mouse recipes and (if you're a mouse family) scratching a tunnel into your room with a view to supplementing the deficiencies of the *en pension* system?

If you're a tortoise, does the management move people into your shell from the annexe?

Let's hope not. Given that what most animals want in this anthropomorphic world is a bit of a break from having to live like human beings, let's pray they get it.

# Portnoy's Jaws, Or For Whom The Great Sound And The Godfather Toll – 22

*With no sign of a let-up in the woodpulp shortage, the Great American Novel for 2077 is actually the Only American Novel for 2077. Care for a few representative extracts?*

AT 10.36 on the morning of July 15, 2071, the Betelgeuse Shuttle took off from Ehrlichman Airport, Savannah, 448 gross tons of di-anylo-polyvectane alloy hurled forward and upward with the incredible thrust of its four Yung & Foolisch oxy-chlorothyne motors.

On the ground, scarce five hog-springs from Ehrlichman control, two Negro dirt-farmers watched the white furrow plough across the hot Southern sky.

'Ah wuz up tuh Miz Golightly's house, yez'day,' murmured Henry Clay Jackson Calhoun. He spat in the dust. He picked a thread out of his age-bleached jeans. He yawned, tongue jumping pink in his large toothless mouth like a plucked rat caught in a storm-drain.

'Miz Golightly with thuh big ole belly?' enquired Washington Bing Beiderbecke Faulkner. He turned a dried cowpat over with his bare black toe. He broke wind. He took off his straw hat and spun it upon his finger.

'Uh-huh,' nodded Henry Clay Jackson Calhoun. He plucked a cotton boll listlessly, and began to pick it to pieces. 'They do say where she carryin' de Devil's chile in that big ole belly o' her'n. It lookin' like she gittin' thuh action f'om Old Nick hisself, heh-heh-heh!'

Washington Bing Beiderbecke Faulkner shook his head.

'It sho lookin' like it fixin' tuh be a bad, bad summer. It like to wipe out thuh entiah crop, white folks liftin' their skirts fo' thuh Prince o' Darkness.'

'Saw a daid toad under a beulah bush this mornin',' said Henry Clay Jackson Calhoun darkly. 'Only mean one thing.'

They stared at a circling yippity-bug for some time. Mule-hooves clopped on the dirt road. They looked up. A bearded figure in a long black coat jiggled in the stained saddle, his sideburns lank in the breezelessness. He came abreast of them.

'Mornin', Rabbi,' said Washington Bing Beiderbecke Faulkner.

The old man took off his yarmulka and wiped his streaming forehead with it.

'All of a sudden it's good morning?' he snapped. 'What for a morning is it, it should be good? What's so good, it should suddenly be a morning? You work, you die, *this* you call life?'

'Saw a daid toad under a beulah bush a bit back,' said Henry Clay Jackson Calhoun.

The Rabbi replaced his yarmulka.

'Schwarzers!' he snorted, deep in his beard. 'They dance, they sing, they get drunk, what do they know?'

'Anything wrong, Rabbi?' asked Washington Bing Beiderbecke Faulkner.

The Rabbi looked at him.

'Anything *wrong*? Anything *wrong*? I forgot to call my mother, he asks me if anything's wrong!'

He dug his slippered heels into the mule's fly-nibbled flanks, and jogged mumbling on. The Negroes watched him go. Henry Clay Jackson Calhoun pulled at his ear-lobe.

'They say he in damn big with thuh Mafia,' he said.

Forty thousand miles up, on the black interstellar threshold, Captain Manuel Garcia y Ortega flicked the anodised oxolium switch .026 ektars to the left.

But nothing happened.

It was 11.34 am.

Senator Seamus Kowalski, firebrand North Dakota Whig, lay on his green leather-topped Washington desk beside his lissom Navajo secretary, pondering defence expenditure in the brief calm stases. The Army was pressing for nuclear revolvers to give them strike parity with the Detroit Police Department, the Navy was screaming for a second Polaris whorehouse for sub-Antarctica, the USAAF wanted in-flight baseball, and, as if this were not enough, his daughter was planning to marry a Jap.

Seamus Kowalski was a homeloving dynast, who had always dreamed of having a son-in-law called Chuck. How could you call a Jap Chuck?

His secretary began to lick his palms. Senator Kowalski frowned. Was this why he had fought his long way to Capitol Hill? Was this what Thomas Jefferson meant when he said that 'When a man assumes a public trust, he should consider himself a public property'?

The red telephone bit, jangling, into his whirling mind. He snatched the instrument from its cradle.

He listened.

He paled.

He gasped.

He rolled from his desk and groped for his socks.

He croaked: 'Leave it with me. Oh my God!' and hung up.

'What up, Keemosabi?' grunted his secretary.

'Take the feather off,' snapped the Senator, removing his own black mask. 'A shark just ate the President.'

A quarter of a million miles away, the Moon receding in his wing mirror, Captain Manuel Garcia y Ortega thought coolly for a few moments, and threw up.


'Eat the chicken soup,' said Mrs Santarosa.

'But we're Mexicans, mother!' protested little Gonzales Santarosa. 'We're wetbacks.'

Mrs Santarosa clipped his ear with the heavy ladle.

'What's so special about Mexicans, they shouldn't eat chicken soup?' she screamed. 'What's so special about chicken soup, it shouldn't get eaten by Mexicans?' She beat her breast, she looked upwards to the ceiling. 'You bring up children, and what do you get? Heartache, you get. A malignant disease, you get.'

Little Gonzales blew his nose on his napkin.

'We're supposed to eat enchelados,' he wailed, 'we're supposed to eat tachos and chili and tortillas!'

'Suddenly he's an expert, my son!' shrieked Mrs Santarosa. 'Suddenly, six years old, he's already a professor!' She put her face down close to his. 'So tell me, you know so much, how many Mexicans ever got to write *Rhapsody In Blue*? How many Mexicans ever ran a blouse empire? How many Mexicans ever got to sell three million copies of *Sonny Boy*? If I started to list the people who got to the top on chicken soup, we'd still be sitting here Sunday week!'

The boy dipped his spoon into the bowl, morosely.

'I liked it when we all spoke Spanish around the house,' he said.

'*Aye, chihuahua!*' cried Captain Manuel Garcia y Ortega, a million miles away. 'We have to re-trim, or we end up in the Sun! We have to lose twelve thousand kilograms right now!'

'I say we throw out the nuns,' said his second-in-command.


'What have you come up with, Senator?' said the two young men from the *Washington Post*.

'We're working on a Second Shark Theory,' said Kowalski. 'As of this moment in time, men, we are into a bi-shark conspiracy situation.'

'You think this shark or sharks had prior information that the President would be swimming off Chappaquiddick?' said the two young men.

Senator Kowalski mopped his neck.

'Let me tell you something about Ivan, boys,' he said. 'God moves in a mysterious way.'

'May we quote you?' said the two young men.

'This conversation is being recorded,' said the Senator 'I think you ought to know that. Similarly, I wouldn't want nothing to get to either of your wives' ears about that big Eskimo stripper.'

There was a long silence.

'I'm afraid there's something you have to understand here, Senator,' said the two young men.

'I thought you might say that,' said Kowalski.

He depressed a foot switch. The door opened. Two large men came in. They had napkins tucked into their collars. Each carried a Chianti bottle. They were still chewing.

The Senator got up and went across, and kissed them both on the lips, very formally, and they turned and beat the two young men to death with the Chianti bottles.

They turned to go.

'Just a minute,' said the Senator.

They turned back.

'What's that stuff on your lips?' he said.

'Issa *tagliatelli alla vongole.*'

'On your way down,' said the Senator, 'send up two orders, easy on the black pepper.'

Two million miles away, ignorant of the deaths of great men, the movements of mighty armies or mighty whorehouses, the racial turbulence of this unsettled Earth, the puzzled nuns floated among the stars.

At the back of the Shuttle, the small man watched them go.

'Cojones,' he said. 'The nuns are only the beginning.'

'I know,' said the big man. 'It will be this thing with the nuns, and then it will be this thing with us.'

'I would like to have run with the bulls at Pamplona one more time,' said the small man.

'Yes,' said the big man, 'the thing with the bulls was better than the green light on the end of Daisy's dock.'

'Fitzgerald was different from you and me,' said the small man

'He had more money,' said the big man

'Apart from that,' said the small man

'Yes,' said the big man

'That is the way it is sometimes,' said the small man

'Yes,' said the big man, 'that is the way it is sometimes '

'When I am floating out there,' said the small man, 'I shall remember you as you were when I first saw you, in the green gingham '

'No,' said the big man. 'The first time, I wore the baby-blue taffeta with the rouched petticoats *You* were in the green gingham.'

'I was in the lamé trouser-suit with the fox stole,' said the small man, 'you stupid bitch '

'Who are you calling a stupid bitch?' said the big man, 'you silly mare '

They were still screaming at one another when Captain Manuel Garcia y Ortega opened the emergency door and threw them out. Love and death, love and death. So it goes

# Schools Fit For Heroes

IT WAS a fine spring morning when I went through what was left of the gate and into the playground of Haringden Comprehensive School, that flawless gem in the Inner London Education Authority's shining crown.

New buds littered the roots of the playground's one remaining tree, fresh frogspawn lay thickly underfoot as jam-jars shattered against little heads, bright paint, still wet, dayglowed its seasonal messages—ROT SHED SWINE, KILL FULHAM PIGS, and so forth—from the flanks of the headmaster's Cortina, and all round me, consonant with the rising sap, shrill screams rose from the rubble as the senior boys went about their morning's rape.

A young master, noticing me out of the corner of his one good eye, rose like Gulliver from the tarmac, shaking the junior children from his clothes. Two of them, teeth firmly bedded in his calves, still hung on grimly as he staggered forward to greet me.

'Hallo,' he said, 'you'll be the, er, wossname, then?'

'Exactly,' I said. 'I am an Educational Correspondent, come to see the workings of the Inner London Education Authority at its best. The debate rages on, you know. What are you doing now?'

'I'm getting beaten up,' he replied. 'We – ow! – we find that the Co-Workers Of Diminished Height like to start the morning off with a few swift kicks at authority, a bit of creative gouging, that kind of thing.'

'You don't mind, then?'

'*Mind?* It is not a—oh my God!—question of minding, brother. It is my duty as a Senior Classroom Operative to see that nothing is allowed to interfere with self-expression. Stop a child kicking your molars down your throat and God knows what irreparable harm you might be doing to his tender psychological fabric.'

Bored at last, his two assailants dropped from his legs and slunk off to stone the school cat. The teacher opened the first-aid satchel chained to his left wrist, and began to dab iodine on his wounds.

'Also,' he said, 'it is all helping to cobble together life's rich lesson. What is a school if not a training-ground for the society that lies beyond it, waiting?'

'True, true,' I murmured. 'What are those little fellows doing up on the gymnasium roof?'

'They are throwing Pakistanis off it,' he said. He gummed a Band-Aid to his seeping knee. 'Yes, here at Haringden we like to think we are kitting out our flock with the psychological, emotional and practical gear necessary to the New Britain of which we are a part. That is why they have broken three of my ribs this week alone: slavish knuckling-under to authority is no preparation for the democratic rough-and-tumble of university or the Trades Union Congress. The knuckle cuts both ways.'

'I see you are a literary man,' I said.

'I done a bit,' he replied. 'I was up at Essex studying arson, and you couldn't help catching the odd phrase or two as the books came past on their way to what I believe has been called the everlasting bonfire.'

'Perhaps we should go over,' I said. 'One or two of the little Asian lads seem to be still alive.'

'It takes all sorts,' said the teacher. 'Yes, he's a plucky bugger, your Gunga Din, I'm not saying he isn't. If he graduates from here in one piece, there's not a segregated Labour Party Club in the country he couldn't kick his way into. OH, WELL PLAYED, LOCKWOOD!'

I turned at his shout to find a tiny boy of perhaps eight kicking a ball between two piles of coats. He had the goalkeeper by the throat and in his wake writhed a number of other boys, clutching themselves at assorted points.

'He'll be captain of Leeds one day,' said the teacher.

'I notice,' I said, 'that the playground has a chalk line down the middle of it. And that children from one half seem not to stray into the other half.'

'You're not slow,' said the teacher, 'I can tell that. Go to

Borstal, did you?'

'Grammar school,' I said, 'as a matter of fact.'

'Oh, we'll have to get you to talk to the kids,' he said. 'They don't see many fascists.'

'About the chalk line?'

'Ah, yes, well, there you have put the finger on the nub, as you might say, of comprehensive education: as you probably know, the main object of the comprehensive system is to bring together children from all social classes and economic groups so that their differences may be more clearly brought out. That way, they learn very early on who their enemies are, and how to continue the class struggle. We find that new kids very rapidly form into gangs with members of their own peer-groups, socially speaking. Every so often a gang from one social class will confront a gang from another social class at the chalk line, and start laying into them. It is what social divisiveness is all about, brother! It is carrying us forward into the 'eighties! It represents the concrete truth behind the abstract concepts of free collective bargaining. It is very democratic: irrespective of intelligence, personality, background, training, or justice, the stronger group invariably wins. I'm thinking of doing a paper on it for *New Society* and going round and hitting the Editor with a brick until he prints it.'

'There appears to be a fight going on there at the moment,' I said. 'Three boys from one side have just jumped a boy from the other side and stolen his purse.'

The teacher stared at me.

'*Fight*, brother?' he said. '*Stolen?* Continuing economic struggle, possibly. Redistribution of income upon a more equitable basis, certainly. We don't want any of your Nazi value-judgements here, mate!'

I glanced at my watch to defuse the threatening acrimony.

'Nearly ten o'clock,' I said. 'Aren't they a little late for class?'

'Not today,' he said. 'They're withdrawing their labour as a gesture of solidarity with the National Union of Railwaymen's pay claim.'

'But the NUR aren't even on strike themselves.'

'Right. *Right!* That's what the lads are trying to avoid, innit? Draw the nation's attention to the sorry plight of the railwaymen while there is still time, brother!'

'Oh. That's rather commendable, in a devious sort of . . . .'

'Can't have the nation's trains grinding to a standstill, can we? No point hanging over a bridge, risking life and limb to drop old prams over and similar when there's nothing coming down the line, is there? Might as well be up the Hendon Flyover firing pellets through juggernaut windows, and that's a ten pee bloody bus ride there and ten pee back, and the way things are these days, you can't tell how long it might take to bash twenty pee out of a little girl. They're getting damned clever at hiding things, the juniors, I can tell you. Look at it from my point of view, there'd be classroom chaos. Life as we know it at Haringden Comprehensive might suffer trauma from which it would never recover.'

'But surely those older boys over there,' I pointed, 'are working on something? They seem to be discussing, writing, all that sort of thing?'

'They're drafting a petition to the headmaster,' he said. 'They want him to send his MA back. Not only does it represent a lickspittle subservience to outmoded academic concepts, it also puts him on a higher intellectual level than them. It is their way of demanding parity. You're looking at a future British Leyland board there, I shouldn't wonder. Or possibly the ship-building industry, if it's nationalised in time. I've never seen a better crop of future British leaders, the combined IQ is only 18, but they'll give you thirty-five per cent of a Whitsunday night shift scale correct to nine decimal places with four pints of Worthington inside 'em and *Match Of The Day* going at full blast in one corner.'

'But what happens to the brighter pupils?' I enquired. 'The, er, cream?'

'They get let out at dinner-time,' said the teacher. 'They look a bit rough, of course, but it's only coal-dust. Best course, really. One clever dick can spoil the whole barrel. Very disruptive, know what I mean!'

'But under the old grammar-school system,' I persisted, 'it was possible for the working-class boy to triumph over social disadvantages by merit and industry and elevate himself to the peak in any area he chose!'

'Absolutely right, brother, wasn't it bleeding disgusting? What chance would the poor sod have in the Britain of the 'eighties? You put your finger right on it, there!' He led me back towards my smouldering car. 'Nice to see your education wasn't entirely wasted.'

# Going Cheep

THIS WEEK, I need hardly say, nine birds have been added to the schedule drawn up under the Protection of Birds Act 1954, that list of feathered items which persons of curious taste may not legally kill, steal, or, for all I know, train to whistle the *Toccata and Fugue in D Minor*.

These birds, as I know you have read, are the short-toed tree-creeper, the little gull, the Mediterranean gull, the gyr falcon, the purple heron, the scarlet rosefinch, the shore-lark, the green sand-piper and Cetti's warbler, and millions of you have written to me in considerable excitement, asking for enough information about them to be able to drop their names with confidence at this weekend's cocktail parties and dole queues.

I have, in consequence and knowing where my professional duties lie, made some investigations, not to say speculations, and am now well able to give you a few salient facts with which to start your conversation off and, I trust, stimulate further ornithological enquiry. To take them in order, then:

## SHORT-TOED TREE-CREEPER

This is a small shifty bird, mottled brown in colour, that hangs around tree roots and sneers at anything that passes. It does not work at all, believing song to be a mug's game, and makes a point of getting up for the dawn chorus only to lean against its roots, examine it claws with studied nonchalance, and occasionally spit out of the corner of its beak. It does not, of course, tear about building its own nests, but squats in those of other birds foolhardy enough to have migrated south without putting their premises in the hands of a reputable agent. It does not go out of its way, in spring, to preen, woo, or otherwise seek a perfect partner, but instead attempts to mate, for form's sake only and out of an instinct it personally finds an irritating drag, with anything it happens to bump into while creeping about. Many have been killed, as a result, by affronted mice, large bees, and the occasional sprightly toad. It is interesting mainly for its supporting role in interminable shaggy-dog stories about Long-Toed Tree-Creepers.

### LITTLE GULL

The little gull is to be found mainly in supermarkets, where it is a sucker for special offers on unlabelled tinned goods. Unlike the Big Gull, which will believe anything it hears about Concorde, North Sea oil, reflation, détente, and so forth, the little gull is conned only by small operations: it will, for example, listen to encyclopaedia salesmen for hours, and often comes home with little things it has picked out of open suitcases in Oxford Street. It is despised by other birds, who are always off-loading unwanted junk on it and, in spiteful mood, telling it tall stories. The little gull, in consequence, believes that the world is flat, and lays its eggs under gooseberry bushes.

### MEDITERRANEAN GULL

The Mediterranean gull is bigger than the little gull (*q.v.*) but no brighter. As its name suggests, it flies to the Mediterranean for the winter, but frequently fails to arrive, since it asks directions from any bird it passes. Mediterranean gulls can, as a result, be found anywhere, at any time of the year; in 1974, three hundred of them spent Christmas in Preston, and a permanent colony now inhabits Tierra del Fuego in the belief that it is Majorca.

Occasionally, however, they do arrive in the Mediterranean, only to discover that they have once more been fooled and that their winter colony is only half-built, miles from the sea, and that they have to sleep twelve to a nest. When they examine the small print in their insurance, they invariably find that they are indemnified only against cycling accidents.

### GYR FALCON

According to p. 788 of the *Shorter Oxford Dictionary* (which I borrowed from a little gull who owned forty-seven copies), the gyr falcon, or gerfalcon, is a native of Iceland, and the *gyr* describes (from the Latin *gyrus*) its habit of flying in circles. From this solid information, we can only induce that it has come here to negotiate, although watch your newspapers for reports that its negotiating circles have widened to two hundred miles in diameter and that it has taken to ramming any English birds found within that limit.

PURPLE HERON
The purple heron is the latest miracle offering from Heron Birds Ltd. Feathered in tasty purple skivertex, with an elegant machine-tooled simulated goldette spine, it spends its life flying into people's homes on ten days' approval, telling them about the sexual passages in Tolstoy. If attacked, its method of defence is to fall apart. Attractive on its own, the purple heron in fact looks best when standing on a shelf with ten others like it.

SCARLET ROSEFINCH
The most intriguing features of this bird are that it is neither scarlet nor a rosefinch. It is more like a large green starling than anything, but not much. Its nomenclature, however, is quite without precedent, and won't happen again, either, if I'm any judge of these matters. Its name was given to it by an ornithologist in debt to a tailor called Sam Rosefinch to the tune of £86. Sam Rosefinch's wife, on the other hand, had always been driven by dreams of show business, and in 1940, following the overwhelming success of *Gone With The Wind*, cut her hair like Vivien Leigh's, changed her name from Lily to Scarlet, and took up drawl lessons. Since there were now three million women in a similar position, Scarlet Rosefinch's career came to nothing, and she went back, in deep depression, to cutting out waistcoat linings. Hearing of this, and instantly seeing it as a way out of his financial difficulties, the ornithologist called on Sam Rosefinch and offered to name his latest discovery after Sam's wife, in return for the £86, plus a spare pair of trousers for his blue worsted. Everyone ended up happy, except for the thing like a green starling, which spends its life answering embarrassing questions from other rosefinches.

## SHORE-LARK

During the week, the shore-lark works in the City and flies home every night to its mate in Wimbledon, where it is a model husband and father. At weekends, however, it migrates briefly to Brighton, on any one of a hundred pretexts, where it meets female shore-larks under the pier and seeks to recapture its lost youth.

## GREEN SANDPIPER

The green sandpiper differs from other sandpipers in that it never learns from its experiences. Many are so green, in fact, that they do not even *have* experiences. In consequence, the male green sandpiper frequently fails to consummate its spring-time relationships, while the female green sandpiper is just as frequently taken down to Brighton by shore-larks. This means that while both the green sandpiper and the shore-lark are understandably rare, and protected, the Greenish Shorepiper is just about the most common bird there is, and shot at all the time.

## CETTI'S WARBLER

Often vulgarly known as the dead warbler, from its habit of sleeping twenty-four hours a day, this bird's correct name was coined in 46 AD, when the Cetti, of Eastern Marathon, were besieged by the Zuccini under their leader Caius Gnocchi the Indecisive. The Cetti, unable to maintain the round-the-clock vigilance necessary to prevent the breaching of their walls, decided to use geese, as was then the custom, for watchdogs. This decision having been taken, the Cetti leaders were then horrified to discover that their geese had been eaten by the starving townspeople the day before. The only birds left in the city were the warblers, who were too small and fiddly to eat. These were gathered up, and stationed at strategic positions on the ramparts, after which the soldiers retired to their desperately-needed rest. That night, the Zuccini mounted their attack, entered the city, and slew the Cetti to a man. The warblers slept through it all.

# Half A Pound Of Tuppeny Vice

*'When police raided the Love Inn, where the Cambridge rapist had been a customer, the owner was alleged to have said: "There is nothing here. This is just a little family sex shop"'* —Daily Telegraph

ON THE KNOTTY rustic lintel beneath the sign of Ye Olde Curiositie Shoppe, the little bell tinkled.

Behind the dusty counter on which lay the dismembered cogs of a cheap Hong Kong dildo into which he was vainly struggling to fit a new mainspring, the proprietor (*Jas. Rumbelow*, ran his copperplate letterheads, *Purveyor of Fyne Thynges to the Gentrie since 1926*) looked up over the gold rims of his bifocals. He laid aside his screwdriver, and beamed.

'Good morning, Mrs Curtoise,' he said.

'Good morning, Mr Rumbelow,' said the customer, a middle-aged lady in a bottle-green swagger coat, lisle stockings, and a hat with three petals missing, 'I was just wondering if you had them gold latex peephole bras and matching suspender belts with the exposé divided-leg panties showing flags of all nations in yet?'

Rumbelow shuffled to the back of the shop, bent over, and shouted down an open trapdoor into the basement.

'Vera, we got any of them Goodnight Las Vegas in a 46?' He turned, on the half crouch, towards the customer. 'It was a 46, wasn't it?'

'Yes. And a 52 hip.'

'And a 52 hip!' shouted Rumbelow, into the darkness.

Scuffling came up through the trap door, counterpointed with spasmodic wheezing and the noise of boxes falling. The stepladder squeaked, and an elderly pink face appeared. A *Penthouse* gatefold was caught in her hairnet by its staple.

'Good morning, Mrs Curtoise.'

'Morning, Mrs Rumbelow. Did you find one?'

Mrs Rumbelow creaked up the last few steps, and into the shop. She shook her head, and the gatefold fluttered to the floor.

'Nearest I come was a 44,' she said, 'but I wouldn't advise it. They give you shocking wind at the best of time, them things. Last thing you want is too small. How about a nice black leather catsuit? I can do that in a 46.'

The customer shook her head.

'Leather doesn't agree with Mr Curtoise,' she said. 'It makes him sneeze in warm weather.'

Rumbelow nodded sympathetically.

'That'll be the tannin,' he said. 'It's like me and rubber, isn't it, Mother?'

'It's like him and rubber,' said his wife. 'We got one of them water-beds off a traveller. A wossname, a sample. Anyway, we filled it off of the upstairs tap, and we got on it, and he was awake all night sneezing, wasn't you? It was like being on the *Titanic*. We was thrown all over the place.'

'I wouldn't have water in the bedroom,' said Mrs Curtoise. 'Call it superstitious, but my old mum used to say "Water in the bedroom, you'll only have girls."'

'I know, I know,' said Mrs Rumbelow. 'I'm the same about lupins.'

'It's a pity about the Goodnight Las Vegas,' said Mrs Curtoise. 'Mr Curtoise'll be ever so disappointed. He put off a Rotary executive meeting specially. I don't know what we'll do tonight, now.'

'There's a new film up the church hall,' said Rumbelow. '*Take Me I'm Scandinavian And My Old Man's On Nights.*'

'We seen it on holiday,' said Mrs Curtoise. 'It's in black and white.'

'What a liberty!' cried Rumbelow. 'There's no pride in workmanship these days.'

'Young people,' sighed Mrs Rumbelow, 'there's no respect.'

'I blame the bomb,' said Mrs Curtoise.

'The Conservatives,' said Rumbelow, 'wouldn't do any better.'

'They're all as bad as one another,' said Mrs Curtoise.

Mrs Rumbelow looked at her.

'I never realised you was political, Mrs Curtoise,' she said.

Mrs Curtoise sighed.

'You got to be,' she said, 'these days. Well, must be off. There's all Mr Curtoise's tights to iron. He likes a nice crease.'

'He wouldn't be an Area Sales Manager,' said Rumbelow, 'if he didn't.'

'Since you haven't got the Goodnight Las Vegas,' said Mrs Curtoise, 'I'll just take a quarter of aphrodisiac toffees.'

Rumbelow shooed the cat away from the confectionery shelf, took down a large jar, unscrewed it, and shook some of its contents into his scale-pan. He watched the needle carefully, added another sweet, filled a paper bag, and flipped it adroitly.

'When you eat them,' he said, handing the bag over, 'don't forget to take your teeth out. They're like bloody Bostik, pardon my French.'

'I know,' said Mrs Curtoise. 'Mr Curtoise thinks they put something in them.'

'Wouldn't surprise me at all,' said Rumbelow. 'Good day.'

The bell tinkled. Rumbelow watched the door swing shut.

'Good job she never took that catsuit,' he· said. 'With her varicose veins, she'd have swolled up something shocking. You'd have to soap her to get her out of it. Like boys' heads in railings.'

'Funny you should say that,' said his wife. 'Only yesterday, man came in, wanted a set of railings to stick his head through. You was out in the smallest room at the time, begging your pardon, Father. So I told him we didn't go in for that sort of thing.'

'Only got so much space, haven't we?' Rumbelow indicated the teetering piles of boxes, the stuffed shelves, the heaps of cellophane-covered books that littered the floor. 'Start catering for all tastes, where will it end? Come in for railings one day, next day it'll be railings *and* small boys already conveniently stuck in 'em.'

'Like that fellow last Tuesday,' said his wife, 'coming in here, big as you please, asking for a packet of Welsh letters. Where do you think you are, I said, Marks and Spencers?'

'Quite right, Mother,' said Rumbelow. 'People today, it's incredible! When my old dad started this business up, you could make a nice little living out of nothing more than a slab of prawns and a half gross of Spanish Fly!'

The bell tinkled again, and a thin fifty-ish man came into the shop, dragging what might have been his misshapen shadow.

'Morning, Mr Collinson,' said Rumbelow. 'What's that you've got there?'

Collinson hoiked the thing up off the floor and draped it over the counter.

'That,' he muttered, and his voice was tense, and his pointing finger shook, '*that* is Miss Mary Wonderful, 38-22-36 When Inflated. Or was.'

'Was?' said Rumbelow.

'Woke up this morning,' said Collinson bitterly, 'and there she was, lying beside me, like a burst inner-tube.'

'Well,' said Rumbelow, 'that's what she, er, was, basically, Mr Collinson.'

Collinson glowered at him.

'That's not what you said when I bloody bought her!' he cried. 'Five-feet-two of delectable rubber pulchritude, you said. Just the companion for those lonely winter evenings, you said.'

'I was reading off the box,' said Rumbelow. 'I don't test 'em all personal.'

'She's perished!' shrieked Collinson. He held up the flaccid corpse, and light shone through its perforated bust. 'My beloved is perished! £14.75, excluding pump, and all I got to show is a load of rubber bands!'

Rumbelow pushed his glasses up onto his forehead and peered at the wreck.

'It looks to me like the dog's been at her,' he said. 'That's never fair wear and tear. You haven't left her lying about, have you?'

'Lying about? LYING ABOUT? What do you take me for? I went to a grammar school. Women have always been treated with utmost respect on my premises! The dog's never off his chain.'

Rumbelow cleared his throat, awkwardly.

'Mr Collinson,' he said, 'you haven't, as it were, bitten her yourself, have you?'

'Bitten her *myself*?' screamed Collinson. 'I wouldn't take such liberties! I hardly know her. I've only had her out of the box twice, to watch *Upstairs, Downstairs* with me. You can't rush things. Call me old-fashioned, but that's how I am. *And* I want my money back!'

'You could patch her,' offered Mrs Rumbelow, who had come back in to feed the parrot, 'couldn't you?'

'Ho, yes, I should bleedin cocoa!' shouted Collinson. 'Very erotic, that! For them as likes nipping into bed with a second-hand bike, it'd be just the thing!' He gathered up the tattered rubber, and stuffed it under one arm. 'That does it, Rumbelow! I have shopped here man and boy—and, for a brief period, woman and girl—for thirty-two years! But from now on, it's the new supermarket for me!'

The Rumbelows reeled! The Rumbelows paled!

'THE NEW WHAT?' shrieked Mrs Rumbelow.

Collinson cackled nastily.

'You heard!' he said. 'Four floors of arcane delights, wall-to-wall wossname, free films, seductive music as you browse at your ease, topless experts to help you with your every enquiry, gratis glossy brochures, cheap travel arranged, money back if not at least partially satisfied—*what do you say to that, you old fleabag?*'

With which Collinson spun on his heel, and strode out, the rubber corpse gesticulating beneath his arm like broken bagpipes.

The Rumbelows stared after him.

'A supermarket!' wailed Mrs Rumbelow. 'All chrome and plastic, cold, impersonal! Cheap, vulgar, American! Nobody giving you the time of day, nobody caring, nobody wanting to know! Where is it all going, Father? What will become of us?'

Rumbelow pressed his face against the window, staring out.

'England, what are you doing to yourself?' he murmured.

# I'm Gonna Sit Right Down And Write
## The Times *A Letter*

THE FIRST CUCKOO, a selection of letters to *The Times* edited by Kenneth Gregory, has just been published at £4.50. Why anyone should, in these dark fiscal days, fork out this sum for a book which does not include my own famous correspondence to that paper and the ensuing hoo-ha, is beyond me. I may write to *The Times* about it. On second thoughts, I may wait until night falls upon the great metropolis and follow Mr Gregory with a sockful of gravel.

On third thoughts, I shall reproduce the entire correspondence in full.

### Intentions of Miss Doreen Nugent
*From Mr Alan Coren*
Sir, I was interested to read (March 8, 15, 20, April 3, 6, May 14) that Mr Bernard Levin is passionately in love with Miss Kiri Te Kanawa, a singer. While I do not know, nor greatly care, what 'Vitae summa brevis spem nos vetat incohare longam' means, may I beg the favour of your illustrious columns to seek the advice of wiser heads than mine in the matter of Miss Doreen Nugent, spinster, of Finsbury Park?

I have been escorting Miss Nugent since August 9, 1970, when I met her at a Czech Wine 'n' Cheese Nite at the Rat and Cockle, Brondesbury. I do not mean, of course, that the wine 'n' cheese was Czech, but the nite was, i.e., it was for Czech people to get together and reminisce. I must add that I am not Czech, nor is Miss Nugent, but entrance was not restricted, and we went upstairs in the first instance to see what the banging on the ceiling was, which turned out to be a hokey-cokey, and we were invited to stay.

Since then, our friendship has blossomed into love; or at least, mine has, but Miss Nugent has taken to sticking her hat pin in my hand when I put it on her knee in the cinema and similar. As five years have passed, I feel I have the right to know what my prospects are: I am 36 years old, with my own 1963 Hillman, and earning a good wage, and I do not suffer from any real diseases to speak of. We both like Austrian food, Ruby Murray records, dogs, and hill-walking, and are opposed to insecticides and slavery. But she tells me that she wants to wait for a better linguist. Should I put my foot down, or start studying odd languages like Tamil, or give her up, or what?

Yours faithfully,
ALAN COREN
23 Tudor Street, EC4.
June 3, 1975.

## Intentions of Miss Doreen Nugent
*From His Excellency the Czech Ambassador*

Sir, May I presume upon your good offices to correct any possible misinterpretation that your esteemed readers might be encouraged to put upon the observations of your correspondent (June 3)?

The so-called meetings that take place at the Rat and Cockle, Brondesbury, do so without any sanction from the Government of the People's Republic of Czechoslovakia. Indeed, the group responsible, which calls itself the Friends of Free Czechoslovakia, is in actuality a neo-Nazi band of fugitive traitors dedicated to the undermining of democracy in Central Europe. It comes as no surprise to me, nor to any freedom-loving person, I am sure, to hear that these fascists think nothing of doing the hokey-cokey with no thought for the comfort or the wishes of others, at the same time masquerading as people who themselves have been subject to unwarranted impositions upon their so-called rights.

Nor can I understand your correspondent's assumption, implicit in the 'of course' of his second paragraph, that there is no Czech wine or cheese. I need only mention the toothsome Slovodny, made from pear pips, and the rich lingering flavour of Osczny Dom, produced from pig's milk, to give the lie to that! To my mind, and to the mind of democratic people everywhere, there is no finer meal than a slice of Slovodny washed down with a sparkling goblet of Osczny Dom.

Yours faithfully,
JANOS BILAK,
25 Kensington Palace Gardens, London, W8.
June 5, 1975.

## Intentions of Miss Doreen Nugent
*From the Bishop of Angmering*
Sir, Am I alone in wondering about the etymology of hokey-cokey?

Yours faithfully,
ERIC ANGMERICTUS,
Slug Cottage, Rustington.
June 8, 1975.

## Intentions of Miss Doreen Nugent
*From Mr Arnold Wesker and others*
Sir, We feel we cannot let pass the comments of your correspondent (June 3) without intervention.

For some years now, we have kept a close watch on the *Births* columns of your newspaper, and we note that since January 1, 1960, the most popular girls' names have been Jane (134,269), Emma (93,426), Lucy (88,042), Charlotte (69,202), and Katherine (54,989). Doreen, however, has appeared only twice.

To us, that seems, well, how shall we say, remarkable!

Yours faithfully,
ARNOLD WESKER,
JOHN MORTIMER,
GLENDA JACKSON,
KENNETH TYNAN,
WAYLAND YOUNG,
TREVOR NUNN,
BRIAN WALDEN,
DONALD SOPER,
PAT ARROWSMITH,
JONATHAN MILLER,
DAVID HOCKNEY.
The Round House, London, NW1.
June 9, 1975.

### Intentions of Miss Doreen Nugent
*From Sir John Betjeman*

Sir, Before the very name disappears forever beneath the imminent avalanche of polystyrene debris and throwaway knickers, may I just record that *Finsbury Park* is one of the loveliest sounds ever to have fallen upon the human ear? That your correspondent (June 3) is also capable of linking it in the same brief epistle with the almost equally euphonious *Brondesbury* marks him, in my view, as a man worthy of our love and respect.

That Miss Nugent seems to prefer a Tamil-speaker strikes me as no small indication of the maelstrom into which this culture is being sucked.

Yours faithfully,
JOHN BETJEMAN,
The Beefsteak Club.
June 11, 1975.

### Intentions of Miss Doreen Nugent
*From Dr A. L. Rowse*

Sir, Hokey-cokey (June 8) is Warwickshire dialect. Originally, it was a children's dance in derision of a local landowner and pervert, Sir Joshua Hoake, on whom Shakespeare based the character of Titus Andronicus.

Yours faithfully,
A L ROWSE,
All Souls' College, Oxford.
June 12, 1975.

### Intentions of Miss Doreen Nugent
*From Mr Alan Coren*

Sir, I'm afraid that none of this (June 5, 8, 9, 11, 12) is much help. Last night, during *The Sound of Music*, Miss Nugent threw my ring over the balcony of the Astoria, Manor House. I grow desperate.

Yours faithfully,
ALAN COREN,
23 Tudor Street, EC4
June 14, 1975.

49

### Intentions of Miss Doreen Nugent
*From the Commercial Attaché to the Jordanian Embassy*

Sir, Surely Mr Coren (June 14) misses the entire point? In his original letter (June 3), he twice spelt 'night' *n-i-t-e*. And he makes no reference whatever to the refugee problems of the West Bank.

Yours faithfully,
HASSAN YOUSEF SARDI,
6 Upper Phillimore Gardens, W8.
June 16, 1975.

### Intentions of Miss Doreen Nugent
*From Sir John Betjeman*

Sir, The Astoria, Manor House! (June 14). Perhaps the last beleaguered survivor of the great picture palace tradition! It had a navy-blue roof with simulated stars, and crenellated battlements, and the foyer was in the manner of a Moorish *yumdukki*, with real goldfish. What days they were, what dear, dead days!

Yours faithfully,
JOHN BETJEMAN,
The Beefsteak Club.
June 17, 1975.

### Intentions of Miss Doreen Nugent
*From Professor J. D. Chaudra*

Sir, What is all this terrible opprobrium, I ask myself, which is being levelled against the Tamil tongue? (June 3, 11). Greatest of the Dravidian languages, could the majestic 12th-century masterpiece, *Periyapuranam* have been written without it? Tell me that, sir! Also, this disturbing business of the hokey-cokey: it has nothing whatever to do with Titus Andronicus, this Doctor Rowse is a fool, I say; he should be struck off, and what is wrong with *nite*, it is perfectly good to my mind.

Yours faithfully,
J. D. CHAUDRA,
Department of Forestry,
University of Madras.
June 19, 1975.

## Intentions of Miss Doreen Nugent
*From the Warden of Cork Synagogue*

Sir, Doesn't Mr Sardi (June 16) mean the *terrorist* problems of the West Bank?

Yours faithfully,
JACK STONE,
12 Farm Avenue, Cork.
June 20, 1975.

## Intentions of Miss Doreen Nugent
*From the Bishop of Angmering*

Sir, I have hesitated for some time before bringing up the matter of Lord Soper's signature to that letter of June 9 (June 9), and I cannot help feeling that this is neither the time nor the place to mention it.

Yours faithfully,
ERIC ANGMERICTUS.
Slug Cottage, Rustington.
June 22, 1975.

## Intentions of Miss Doreen Nugent
*From Miss Doreen Nugent*

Sir, I knew he was bloody mad all along. Tamil, Glenda Jackson, Arabs, throw-away knickers, live goldfish, where's it all going to end? Imagine if we'd had kids!

Yours faithfully,
D. NUGENT (MISS),
7 Stalingrad Mansions, N4.
June 23, 1975.

# Dancing On The Ceiling

AT 9.10 AM on Thursday, May 6, 1976 (this is a magazine of record, Reader: bear with me for the sake of unborn generations. Pale young men in curious clothes will sit, an eon hence, and pore over bound volumes of this stuff en route to doctorates, when you and I are dust), I was walking along Farringdon Road, at my back King's Cross and on the luminous horizon, Ludgate Hill.

It was an impeccable spring day, warm, cloudless, soft: a day in total empathy with its great events, a climate matched to augury as a cravat to socks. Pathetic fallacy was rife: at that auspicious moment when the Government and the TUC jointly announced agreement on the four-pound ceiling and joyous bells rang out across the land, much in the manner of the finale of *Cinderella*, the sun rose bright and snails poked out their horns, and larks shot chortling into the vernal welkin.

I had listened to the news on the eight o'clock radio, and there was little doubt that this was one of the most important days since the beginning of the world: a country which, only a day or two before, had been written off as ungovernable was now an exemplar to the world of social and political decorum; a currency which, at the beginning of the week, was plummeting fast against Kleenex would now, I gathered, make gold look insecure; an industrial complex which, when I had gone to bed, no one would ask to mend a fuse had suddenly, this morning, started a nervous shiver running down the global spine from Tokyo to the Ruhr.

Funny thing, history.

It was as I, citizen of the imminent New Empire, was about to pass under Holborn Viaduct, dizzily speculating on the fact that four quid could be a fulcrum upon which a universe balanced, that I happened to look at a man who was sprinkling sand from a polythene bag onto an oil-slick behind his lorry. On the side of the vehicle ran the legend BROADS BUILDERS MERCHANTS.

Catching my glance, the man said:

'Lucky I had this on.'

'Right,' I said.

'Very nasty, oil. Someone comes out sudden, put your brakes on, where are you?'

'Quite.'

'Very lucky I had this on,' he said again; and went on sprinkling.

Now, I have to be careful here. I do not want to either lose you, or, worse, have you ringing your Local Authority to inform them that there is a madman loose. But when the man said that it was lucky that he was carrying sand, it immediately struck me that the sand had come a long way to its appointment with destiny in Farringdon Road. It had been a rock, and silently watching, at that fateful far moment when an inorganic molecule, bored with its prospects and more ambitious than its siblings, had taken the decision to go organic; a process which had resulted, some time later, in there being a man to sprinkle on Farringdon Road the sand into which that rock had eroded. It had been about when short hirsute persons had rolled a round stone to the top of a hill and noticed that it rolled down again, a process that had resulted, some time later, in there being a lorry to bring the man to Farringdon Road to sprinkle the sand. It had also been around while all sorts of events had taken place which had no (measurable) bearing on Farringdon Road, e.g. Christ either walking or not walking on the water, Kit Marlowe getting stabbed in a pub in Deptford, Amundsen reaching the South Pole, Ben Lyon discovering Marilyn Monroe, and so on.

Also to be dealt with was the future of the rock/sand, and the alternative future that would now *not* be, because of the rock/sand. That is to say (1) Where would the sand go from here, down what drain, to what destination in, for example, 27,839 AD? and (2) If the sand had *not* been here in Farringdon Road on May 6, 1976, would some vehicle have skidded on the oil, and killed someone whose descendant seed, incalculable years from May 6, have written something better than the Bach Double Violin Concerto or brought democracy to Betelgeuse or found a way of turning base metal into gin?

In short, when the lorry-driver said: 'Lucky I had this on,' should I have answered 'Right'? Suppose the person who would have been killed when the vehicle that might have skidded on the oil which might not have been sanded had turned out to be the progenitor of future Hitler triplets?

All this went through my head in a mere millisecond, and when you consider how many milliseconds there are in a lifetime, you will begin to see that I was starting to have difficulty in taking the four-pound ceiling seriously. *Sub specie aeternitatis*, it was taking on the lineaments of somewhat small beer.

Especially as, less than two minutes later and only a hundred or so yards further south along Farringdon Road, I passed a blackboard outside Oddbins, the wine merchants. On the blackboard, in white-chalk capitals, was written: FREE SHERRY-TASTING TODAY; and beside the blackboard, three tramps were queuing. Now, there are spry journalists around who would have seen this as a golden opportunity to glean their views on the history-shaking deal which had just concluded. But could I, fresh from enquiring about the priorities of sand and ceilings in the great scheme of things, even begin to consider approaching them? Of course not, they were living for the opening of Oddbins; the entire solar system, its past and its future, were contained in a sherry glass. Was the vision of an inflation-rate's prospective fall to 6 per cent by the winter of 1977 part, to them, of life's rich woof?

I smiled at them, though (spring sun is infectious); but they did not respond at all, their eyes were distant. I assume they were savouring past tastes in their memories, measuring Creams against Finos and Olorosos, like three very poor relatives of Orson Welles.

It was at this point that I decided to enter the Dunkin' Donut at Ludgate Circus, read my *Daily Telegraph* very closely over a cup of coffee, and work out exactly what I would write about the immemorial four-pound-ceiling decision in the leader column for this magazine an hour or so later.

I was very, well, conscientious about this mission. It is not every day that the world takes a sudden upward turn and one's children's futures are underwritten by practical seers like Len and Denis; and I was determined to write lucidly about this portent and not to be sidetracked into valueless speculations about man's life on this planet which were in danger of being sparked off by the fact that what I was eating with my coffee was an apple-donut, full of side-alleys in which people like Isaac Newton lurked, and William Tell, and Adam and Eve, and . . .

Assiduously, I read that 'after allowing for the extra tax concessions plus the unconditional extra child allowance of £60 per child allowed in advance in the Budget, the Treasury calculates that a married man with two children under eleven earning £30 per week gross will be £3.16 better off, whereas at £80 a week the net gain has risen only to £4.05' and so on, until the end of the page; and I had got it all pretty straight. And I followed it with lots of excited stuff from politicians and correspondents and fiduciary hot-shots, and I finished my coffee, and would have gone straight to the typewriter, except that I hadn't finished my cigarette and so I turned idly to the insignificant matter of the inside pages.

MY NIGHT WITH BLONDE DESCRIBED BY COAL OFFICIAL, said the page 3 headline. I read the first paragraph. 'A middle-aged balding National Coal Board production manager told the jury in the Sex-For-Bribes trial at Glasgow yesterday of the night he spent with a strawberry blonde model in the Excelsior Hotel at Glasgow Airport after they had been wined and dined and provided with a room by Rotary Tools.'

The strawberry blonde's name was Miss Anna Grunt.

The story beside this (I will not expatiate upon the Rotary Tools/Anna Grunt saga; when I tell you that she had originally been approached at the Crazy Daisy Restaurant, you will realise that it would do none of us any good to proceed further into this labyrinth) was headlined SHOPGIRL WAS FIRED BECAUSE SHE COULDN'T SMILE ALL DAY, and, since the *Telegraph* has a poor sense of climax, concerned a shopgirl who was fired because she couldn't smile all day. She was fired by Miss Joy Churn of the Subway Boutique, Wolverhampton, a spot which, the Court heard, had been left by about forty girls in six months.

Before the mind, still shell-shocked from the blonde infiltration of the Coal Board, strayed too far into visions of this weird subterranean rendezvous through which an unending procession of gloomy girls passed before disappearing God-knows-where (are there tunnel walls beneath Wolverhampton where Dante is doomed to call to Beatrice in flat Brum accents for all eternity?), I made to fold the paper briskly, pay the bill, and move to the aforementioned business of the day. But as I did so, the eye caught a further headline on that same page 3: ACTRESS WENT HOME TO MUM AFTER NUDITY ROW.

Too late! How could I not read on? Like the Ancient Mariner, the *Telegraph* plucked at my sleeve with its wizened columns. This time, Miss Marilyn Galsworthy, up on a charge of wilfully bleaching the clothes of Miss Suzanne Butterfield, the lady who had replaced her in the bed of a Mr Meek, estate agent in the Borough of Camden, was said by Mr Meek to have left the flat they had shared and gone to her mother in Brighton after a row in which he and she had divided on the matter of her showing her bottom during the performance of a play based on the life of Balzac.

I let the paper fall from my numb fingers, and wandered out into Ludgate Circus.

It was only a few hundred yards to my office. I would, I said to myself (I may, by this time, have said it to passers-by) go to that office and write about how history had been changed that day, how life was all about the four-pound ceiling on wages, how events of incalculable significance had taken place, how none of us should ever be quite the same again, and how proper it was for those involved to treat it all so seriously.

I am not, however, entirely sure that that point has really come across.

# Un Cottage De Weekend

'. . . so when Gilbert had such a *succès fou* with his *Trotsky And Hancock: Parameters Of Caring*, twelve impressions and the Prix Chomsky, we thought, well *I* thought—you know Gilbert, give him a few weeks on a narrow boat each year and his Sunday soccer on Primrose Hill and he's perfectly happy with Highgate—I thought it would be rather nice to splash the Canadian rights on a little place in France, *un chaumière*, or is it *une*, a small farmhouse, perhaps, a *pied-à-terre*.

For weekends, short trips, half-terms, all that kind of thing.

Somewhere in the centre, somewhere *tout rural*, away from, well, English cyclists in Halford anoraks, if you know what I mean, and those terrible people in white Rovers who always leave the *Guide* on the table, even in the most fearful hamburger places. Did you see *Une Partie de Campagne*, by the way, all those wonderful vests, those forearms, you could smell the earth. That's what we were after. Not the Dordogne, of course, it's become so common, you see louvred doors being delivered to even the tiniest villages, we passed through one once and Gilbert spotted five different faces from telly commercials, and they were all wearing new berets and waving *baguettes* terribly ostentatiously, I'm sure none of them ever opened a book in his life.

Their children had tee-shirts with pictures of Wagner on them.

Lot-et-Garonne is really the only place to be, you know. The naturalness of it. *Le sans-souci*, as we say down there. Our little *ferme* used to be the village pesthouse, you know; you can still see where sufferers from scrofula banged holes in the foundations with their heads, because Gilbert chipped away all the plaster and exposed the original cell walls, he's truly wonderful with rough tools, once he's out of an academic environment.

Man is naturally a maker, after all, and none more so than Gilbert; he treats reason as a livelihood, no more than that.

He is both Rousseau *et rousseauisme*, if you follow me.

I'm the same. I make a rough *terrine* when I'm down there exactly as it has been made for eleven centuries, you steam the live rabbits then jump on them in clogs just before they're completely asphyxiated, and then dice them with a *sauve-pichet*, it's a kind of single-headed axe. I bake my own bread, too, and Gilbert has an arrangement with a local vineyard, he pays five francs a cask for a wonderful black wine, the locals use it for shrivelling head-lice, I believe it may have something to do with their religion, their observances are quite medieval at times.

We encourage it, where we can. There's a terrible danger of their wonderful primitive spirit being overtaken by *le super-marketisme*, I have seen young women carrying frozen *haricots*; many of the houses have central heating, although Gilbert is doing something about it, he got together with a few close friends in the village and they tarred and feathered the heating engineer, I don't think he'll come back. It was quite a victory. Gilbert can be very dominant, you know, he's very different down there from the way he is in lectures, he wears studded wristbands. We never take deodorants down there. I let my armpits flourish, too; it puts us in touch. *C'est très engagé*.

April is our favourite time of year, the children can help with the slaughtering. Little Cordelia has been butchering lambs ever since she was old enough to wield; it's one of the things missing in progressive boarding schools, I sometimes feel one can have too much Idries Shah and Jerome Robbins, don't you? The twins have neck-wringing races with the chickens, they're such enthusiastic boys! They dance the *pisanne* nude, well we all do, it's a wonderfully stimulating local dance celebrating the sexual energies of the hog. Pig-farming is so important down there, sow-fertility is never far from one's thoughts. We introduced the *pisanne*, as a matter of fact, we thought it was about time the region had its own dance, the locals took it very well, they don't all join in, of course, at least not yet, but they all come along and clap and hoot when we dance it for them.

It may be the rhythm of the *pisanne* that's behind the awakening of sexual experiment down there. That and the fact that we've been distributing the pill, and holding seminars on Oriental concepts; well, Gilbert felt that the Roman Catholic church was repressing natural peasant instinct, strangling it, even. I think they're happier, now.

We are, certainly. It's marvellous to have this completely alternative world to escape to, away from professorial responsibilities, and agents, and accountants, and TV interviews, and dinner parties, all the well-dressed chatty dreariness of the whole London bit . . .

France is so civilised, I find.'

# Son Of Sons And Lovers

WALTER MOREL trudged brokenly up the mean weed-infested alleyway between the coalstained back-to-backs. Beneath the ragged trousers tied at the knee, legs that had once been slabs of ferric muscle were bowed now, corded and varicose; beneath the patched jacket, the spine curved, bowed by the unrelieved labour of the years, and the deep chest heaved and crackled with the effort of pushing one broken boot after the other. The knotty hands, black with a permanent black that defied all scrubbing, swung ineptly; his battered lunch-tin banged along the sagging railings

The alley echoed with the twilight din of cisterns flushing erratically in their corrugated outhouses as Morel turned into his tiny garden, he glanced at the crops struggling pitifully in the mean sod.

'Mean sod!' he muttered, kicking a weeny dune upon which a lettuce, no bigger than a radish-sprout, faltered. The dune collapsed in dust, the lettuce died.

There would be no dinner Saturday, then.

He lifted the rusty latch, pushed open the back door, pulled off his boots, dropped them on the stone floor. He hung his threadbare cap upon its nail, and his jacket beneath it, and his paper collar beside that, and shuffled into the scullery on his calloused sockless feet. The tin bath was ready, as it always was, in front of the fireplace, the scrubbing brush floating in it like a dead hedgehog, the carbolic soap reeking above the smell of the shinbone stew bubbling on the stove.

His wife filled the bath from a pail.

'Tha'd best git in while 'er's hot,' she said. 'Thur's nobbut cold, else.'

Walter Morel took off his wide belt and braces and his trousers and his long underwear, and got in the bath, and sat down.

She looked at his bent back, white, tired, remembered its whip and wire in the time of their joint fires, not so many years ago. Mrs Morel was forty-five, looked sixty; her hair hung in grey whorls from its cheap pins. She glanced at her reddened hands as they soaped her husband's wide blanched back; they looked like lobsters running across tripe.

''Ow wur it oop t'bank, then, Walter?' she enquired, as she always did.

'Sem as yesdy,' grunted Morel, 'an' sem as t'morrer'll be. Bank's allus bank. They cooms in fer t'pay, they cooms in wi' daft bloody questions about overdrafts, they cooms in after financial bloody advice an' what ter do wi' stocks an' shares an' mortgages an' they parks their bloody great Volvos all over t'shop an' they treats me like nobbut dirt, sem as always. Ten year ah bin bank bloody manager, an' nivver a bloody one as calls me owt but bloody surname. An' ah grovels an' tooches bloody forelock an' says "Yes sir" an' "No sir" an' "Three bags bloody full sir". Miners!' he roared suddenly, sluicing the grimy water down his chest. 'Miners, wi' their airs an' bloody graces an' their silk bloody shirts an' their furrin cars! Miners, wi' their eight bloody hours a week in t'pit an' two hunnerd poun a week after stoppages! Miners, wi' their la-di-da bloody voices an' "Should we have a little flutter on Marks and Sparks this month, Morel?" an' "I say, Morel, the wife and I were thinking of a week or two in Antibes, lay on a few francs, there's a good chap!" Miners!' he spat, finally, into the encircling suds.

'Tha'll need t'Brillo for t'hands,' said his wife, quietly. 'Ah'll get 'er.'

'Nay, moother,' said Morel, 'tha'll not get ink out wi' Brillo, 'er's ingrained, tha knows. Ah'll joost tek me tea, an' be off wi' Charlie.'

'Whippets tonight, is it, Walter?'

'Naw, naw, tha daft bogger! Whippets is Wednesday, tonight's t'Rotary, tha knows, we're tekkin on t'Conservative Association Pigeon Team!'

He rose, creaking, from the tub, and began to towel himself with half an old blanket. An untypical smile broke out briefly on his lips.

'Aye, our pigeons 'as a damn good chance tonight, lass! We

nivver beat Conservatives yet, but seein' as 'ow they 'ad to eat three o' their best birds at las' week's Annual Dinner An' Ball, we should see 'em off proper!' He rubbed his hands together gleefully. 'By 'eck, ah've joost remembered, t'Masonic Lodge is having a Ladies' Dinner Friday night, wi' a bit o' luck they'll be a couple o' whippets short for next week's area semi-final, hee-hee-hee!'

He drew his rags back over his racked frame, took a swig of ebony tea, and, stuffing the wedge of bread-and-scrape into his jacket-pocket, opened the door just as his son Paul was about to step through it into the house.

His father looked at him; or, rather, up·and down him. The old banker's lip curled.

'Got a white shirt on, then?' he said. 'Look at them hands, mother, like a girl's, soft as bloody butter, reet miner's hands he's got. Son o' mine wi' reet bloody miner's hands!'

'I wish they were,' said Paul, seventeen and slim as a flute, dark doe-eyed and the soft hair falling about his shoulders like a pre-Raphaelite martyr.

His father clipped his ear, or at any rate the ringlets over it, with the back of his knuckly hand.

'Bin 'anging round wi' bloody miners again, has tha?' he roared. 'Bank people not good enough, is that it?' He leaned forward, and a menacing forefinger jabbed the boy's frail ster- num. 'Tha'll git nobbut swillikins in yer gawpie wi' they minin' nobs, lad! Tha'll mek thissen a laffin' stock, soockin' oop t'miners, they'll never let thee near a pit, let alone down 'er. Did tha nivver 'ear about closed shop, sonny boy? You keep to yer station in life, my lad, you know yer place! My dad wur a banker, an' 'is dad wur a banker before 'im, in the good days, when bein' a bloody banker meant summat, when folks looked oop t'bankers, when it wur a reet craft. An' now ah'm a banker, too, and tha'll be a bloody banker an' all, if ah knows owt about it! Morels 'as allus gone down t'bank, an' allus will!'

Whereupon he shoved the boy aside, strode furiously through the rickety slat-door, and hurled it shut behind him. Mrs Morel looked at her son. She pushed a wisp of hair back into its misshapen bun. He had always been her favourite.

'Tha's caught me off-guard, son,' she murmured, coy, dropping her gaze. 'Ah've not a bit o' rouge about me, an' thee coomin' straight off t'Top.'

Paul smiled. The Top, that glittering hill of emerald lawns and split-level executive two-car-garage homes, was the elite part of the town where the mining classes lived, drinking their vodkatinis by the private putting-greens while their Filipino couples buffed the tumble-driers to an immaculate sheen. It was said the colour televisions were never switched off.

'How do you know about that, mummy?' said Paul.

Despite her love for the boy, his mother blanched.

'By the right, son, if tha dad ever 'eard tha talk like that, 'e'd 'ave his belt off to thee! Tha's mixin' too much wi' miners' sons, tha's pickin' oop their Etonian ways, it'll be beagling next.'

'Not just their sons, mummy,' murmured Paul.

'Tha what?'

'There's a girl—'

'Girl? You mean—'

'Her name,' said Paul, looking out of the window, 'is Fiona Gormley-Gormley!'

Mrs Morel reeled! She fell back against the mantelpiece, and the little jam-jars of loose-change jumped and jingled. Her mouth fell open, and the firelight winked off her NHS tin dentures.

'*Fiona Gormley-Gormley?*' she shrieked. 'Tha's never walking out wi' Fiona Gormley-Gormley? 'Er dad's a foreman face-worker, lad, he teks home nigh on a grand a week, they've a week-end place in Eton Square an' a steam yacht lyin' off Montego Bay, full o' free coal! They sits down reg'lar at table wi' Lord Scargill an' the McGahey o' McGahey. Folk say as 'ow her father fans his tea wi' a mink cap!'

'I—I can't help it, mummy, it's jolly hard to describe but when I'm with Fiona a sort of inferno roars through my loins and Fiona says that she has these enormous waves breaking on the shore that thunder through her in unremitting surges and break upon her innermost recesses. Is that love, mumsy?'

'Is it boggery! Love is going to Young Conservative fêtes together an' mekkin' sure yer betrothed 'as a pensionable position wi' luncheon vouchers an' gets out of 'is bath when he wants a widdle. Ah'm talking' plain, Paul, as talkin' plain's me nature. What's wrong wi' girls round here, son, girls of our own class, decent middle-class lasses from old stockbroking families, brain-surgeons' daughters, solicitors' girls? Poor as church mice they maun be, but brass isn't everything, lad. Stick to yer own sort, there's nobbut grief for a banker's boy up t'Top!'

Paul opened his mouth to protest, but the words died unuttered. For at that very second, there rang through the mean little streets that terrible banshee wail of sirens that drove like a fearful spike into the hearts, nay the very souls, of all who struggled for life within its dreary compass! And, as ever, hardly had the grim electric screaming died away than its echo was taken up by the yet more awful cries of women and children and, yes, even the men themselves.

Mrs Morel, snatching her black shawl about her, ran from the door, her son on her heels, and into the narrow street already crowded with a hurtling throng of neighbours, whose clogs clattered upon the uneven cobbling like the death rattle of the Earth itself. Down the steep hill they ran, towards the last dying notes of the tocsin.

'A disaster at t'bank!' they cried as they ran. 'A disaster at t'bank!'

When the Morels got to the bottom of the hill, the bank's façade was hidden by the weeping mob. Middle-class members from t'Bottom, lawyers, doctors, retirees on small fixed incomes, shopkeepers, managers, businessmen of every description shrieked and beat their breasts, while the bleak wind carried off their torn hair, blowing the pitiful tufts hither and yon in a bitter little game all its own.

The bank, of course, had long closed for the day; but where else were the relatives of the victims to run? For on the six o'clock news, the grim tidings had broken, that, as the result of collapsed pay-talks, freezes, contracts, understandings, union and CBI agreements, and the latest of that year's eighteen Government revolutionary incomes policies, the £ now stood at eighteen cents.

And so clamorous was the grief of the stricken middle-class victims (and, it has to be said, so muted was the purr of the Bentley engines), that none of them even heard the sound of the miners driving down from t'Top to their branch HQ to put in those wage-claims which were, after all, the only hedge against inflation open to them.

# A Short History Of Insurance

1. THE DAWN OF INSURANCE

It is impossible, naturally, to fix a date for the birth of insurance; but most authorities agree that it was probably discovered by accident, the favoured theory being that our early ancestors found, upon rubbing two sticks together, that their tree burned down.

There are also cave-paintings which show men running after buffalo, and some anthropologists maintain that the men are attempting to interest the buffalo in a policy insuring them against extinction, while the buffalo are running away on the grounds that they already carry enough insurance, but this is at present only informed speculation.

2. INSURANCE IN THE NILE DELTA

Around 5000 BC, the first Egyptian and Mesopotamian settlements were founded. Their inhabitants were roughly divided into two kinds: those who thought that, after death, you came back as a cat; and those who thought you didn't come back at all. As a result of this, life insurance took two forms: the normal With Profits policy, by which the family of the bereaved were guaranteed, on his death, a continuous supply of fish; and, a new invention, an Annuity maturing in old age which provided the insured with gold pots, pans, spoons, etcetera which he could put in his sarcophagus to await his demise, whereupon they would all cross The Great Divide together and he could set up home in some style.

As you know, many of these tombs were subsequently robbed, usually by the families who had only been left fish.

3. THE POLICIES OF THE ALMIGHTY

It was about this time, too, that the Children of Israel first appeared on the insurance scene, introducing the myriad complications that remain to this day and which gave original rise to the All Risks Policy. As you know, the Almighty (in an uncharacteristic lapse from His infinite wisdom) gave an early assurance to His people of overall cover, not realising at the time that they were as accident-prone a race as you could come across in a month of Sundays, all right, Saturdays.

As a consequence, He was constantly intervening in their disordered lives in a desperate running attempt to remain solvent: had Noah's family not had advanced warning of unseasonal weather, for example, the compensation would have been astronomical, and who would have thought when assessing the actuarial odds and thereby arriving at a negligible premium, that someone would actually end up in the belly of a whale? Exegeticists who have sought explanations in natural law for the parting of the Red Sea need look no further, once they have totted up the pay-out on forty thousand accidental drownings. The Egyptians, of course, were not covered for the loss of their entire armed forces, and are still, sixty centuries later, trying to catch up. Even now, the Russians will not cover them in the event of TK-47's being taken any nearer than twenty kilometres from deep water.

The result of these early experiences has been, in our day, the Act Of God designation on all insurance policies; which means, roughly, that you cannot be insured for the accidents that are most likely to happen to you. If your ox kicks a hole in your neighbour's Maserati, however, indemnity is instantaneous.

4. THE FIRST GOLDEN AGE
"'The hour of departure has arrived, and we go our ways – I to die, and you to live. Which is the better, God only knows.''

And with these words, Socrates bade them remove from him, and they went apart in sorrow and left him. And when a messenger came to tell them that Socrates was dead, they stood about, and many wept, and Glaucus, senior of the disciples and most beloved, uncovered his face at last and said:

"One good thing, there's a policy in my name."

And Epidomus said:

"That's better than a poke in the eye with a sharp stick."

But in the late forenoon, Socrates's broker came to Glaucus

and said that he was sorry to have to inform him that, Socrates having taken his own life with a draught of hemlock, the policy was null and void. He then referred Glaucus to Section Four, Paragraph Nine.

Whereupon Glaucus turned upon him in rage and argued that Socrates had not committed suicide voluntarily but had been directed to do so by the State.

So the broker referred Glaucus to Section Eight, Paragraph Five.

And Glaucus beat his breast and cried:

"I have sat at that old bugger's feet these thirty years when I could have been out enjoying myself, and I have never understood a bloody word he said, and now you tell me I was on a hiding to nothing, what kind of business are you running here?"

And the broker said:

"Glaucus, in a republic, do we feel it advances the good to allow benefit to accrue to the bad even though the bad are beyond the advantage of the benefit and have therefore endowed the benefit to the good?"

And Glaucus said:

"You know what *you* can do."'

PLATO, *Apologia*

5. MOTOR INSURANCE IN THE FIRST CENTURY AD
When King Prasutagas died in AD 61, the territory of the Iceni was violently annexed by Rome, and his queen, Boudicca, was raped. Enraged, Boudicca raised the whole of South-East England in revolt against their Roman conquerors, fitted scythe-blades to the wheels of her army's chariots, and drove them through the ranks of her enemies.

Subsequently apprehended and charged with (1) Exceeding XVIII mph in a built-up area, (2) Driving without due care and attention, and (3) Failing to observe the right of way, Boudicca was then issued with some three thousand writs for actual damages by solicitors acting on behalf of the maimed Roman infantry.

Upon contacting her insurance company, she was informed, regretfully, that by making modifications to her vehicles without previously informing the company of her intention to do same, the company had no other course but to declare invalid the Third Party liability. The subsequent proceedings resulted in a bill for damages amounting to £8,731,267, a sum utterly beyond the reach of the British, who, then as now, had only the woad they stood up in.

The Romans thought about this for a bit, and decided that their best course of action would be to annihilate the British somewhere between London and Chester.

An interesting sidelight on this affair is that the Romans also learned a lesson from it, which was that the chariot need not be just a way of getting you there and bringing you back, but also a weapon in its own right. Even today, only 19% of pedestrians setting out to cross the Via del Corso get to the other side.

### 6. 1066: THE GREAT LEAP FORWARD

Insurance came of age on the beach at Hastings, when King Harold, who carried today's equivalent of £100,000 in Personal Disability insurance, was shot in the eye by a Norman bowman firing through a narrow slit in the defence wall.

His queen immediately contacted the insurance company, enclosing a plan as required by the claim form showing the path of the arrow. The insurers examined the policy for some days and were growing desperate at their inability to find a way of legitimately welshing on the deal when one of their younger colleagues noticed a gap in the defences, which were, of course, Harold's responsibility.

'Here,' he said, 'if that wasn't there, the arrow'd never have got through!'

And thus it was that *loophole* entered the history of insurance, since which time it has gone from strength to strength.

### 7. THE MODERN ERA

The Modern Era, or Golden Age, of insurance can be said to have been ushered in by the birth, in 1623, of Josiah Smallprint Son of a Lincolnshire pharmacist, young Josiah spent his early years amusing himself among his father's alembics and phials. It was thus, on November 18, 1641, that he stumbled upon an ink which could be put onto paper by type, but which remained invisible until the paper was put at the back of a drawer Upon removing the paper from the drawer and examining it again, the owner found it to carry all sorts of information hitherto un-noticed

The first example of Josiah's handiwork to be used commercially was the phrase '   . always provided that a pig flew past at the time the accident occurred'

There is a statue to Josiah, 1st Baron Smallprint, in the foyer of Policymonger's Hall

# The Ford Papers

*As the 38½th President of the United States disappeared into the political sunset, his thoughts turned naturally towards the composition of that mandatory ex-Presidential volume, his* Memoirs. *This is the first draft of the complete book. I did the spelling.*

CHAPTER ONE: A DATE WITH DESTINY
It was, I think, my great predecessor Warren Harding who kept saying 'Here's another fine mess you've got us into, Stanley,' and there have been times when I knew exactly what he meant.

This doesn't seem to be one of those times.

I can't remember who Stanley was, either; it was probably Harding's Vice-President, I guess. One thing I do know, their car kept falling apart.

Well, it has been said that few are called but only many are chosen, and when they came to tell me I was President of the United States, I was looking for my blue cap out back in this yard we had at the time. It never did turn up; so much intervened, South East Asia, Hirohito's state visit and having to eat fried seaweed, going to Helsinki and forgetting my brown brogues, still, I guess it'll be where I left it, and now there's time on my hands, I'll ask around, you never know with caps.

It was in August 1974 they came to me and said that President Nixon had decided to resign; I was amazed, he was at the height of his popularity, and he had always been very civil to my wife and myself, all I could think of was he had been offered a better job. After all, he was no chicken, you have to think about your future these days, I am always trying to get this across to people. Anyway, I told them I was very happy for the Nixons and hoped a house went with it, and I gave them five dollars towards the barometer which I guessed was why they had come by, and I told them I would serve the new President to the best of my ability. They all laughed at that, I guess they were feeling tense, or something; then it hit me. It was I they was talking about! I remember running into my wife Carol, Betty, and shouting 'I'm the new President, let's go to a movie and eat Chinese after!'

## CHAPTER TWO: THE GUYS ON THE TEAM

I swam a lot that Fall. One of my clearest memories of those first weeks in office is the backstroke. You do it with your face looking up, as opposed to down, and not everyone can do it on account of you crack your skull against the side all the time, and unless you're pretty damned careful, it can cost you a whole lot of money in tiling. I'm lucky, due to I know this decorator from the old days in Grand Rapids, he gets twenty per cent off all sundries of that nature.

Anyhow, I put together a really hot cabinet, Ted Levi had been the President of the University of Chicago, John Dunlop was an economics professor at Harvard, F. David Matthews had been President of the University of Alabama, and Hank Kissinger and Jim Schlesinger also had a lot up here, as everyone knows. It was terrific just listening to them talk, like going to one of them black-and-white movies.

I guess I have to admit that I got off to a pretty shaky start in foreign affairs, partly owing to where I had ripped the map pages out of my Captain Marvel Diary For 1974 to clean my pipe. This happened before I was President, of course, I would not do such a dumb thing now; this explains why I had such a tough time with Congress over military aid to Cambodia in 1974, I think they lost a little confidence in my strategy after I told them I planned to drive down that afternoon and see the place for myself. I waved the sandwiches to show I didn't intend to blow money in expensive restaurants while I was there, and some of the old guys fainted.

Right after that, the Cambodians retaliated by seizing the *Mayaguez*, and I sent in the Marines. This was hailed, as you know, as a masterstroke of positive strategy and sent my popularity way up at home; I didn't understand this, on account of sending in the Marines was all I could think of, I had always thought that was what you did if you were the President, I had

seen *Sands of Iwo Jima* fourteen times, and the Marines won *every
single time*! Why mess around with a winning formula, is my
motto.

CHAPTER ONE AGAIN: I REMEMBER ABOUT THE BLUE CAP
I remember about the blue cap. I used it to plug the gas-filler in
that old Studebaker I used to run. Boy, that's a relief, I'm pretty
attached to that cap, I wore it the night I walked into a tree on
Elm Street, Spokane!

All I have to do now is remember what I did with the
Studebaker.

CHAPTER THREE, OR MAYBE FOUR: ANOTHER DATE WITH
DESTINY
In September, 1974, I pardoned Richard Nixon. It was a
controversial decision, I understand, but I don't see why.
Anybody can take a better job, it's just they get so damned
offended in Washington, I'll just bet nobody else shelled out a
whole five bucks

That winter, I studied hard on foreign affairs, which
everyone said was my weak spot, personally I reckon it's a hell
of a lot better than my breaststroke, but there you go, people are
funny. It was good I boned up on foreign affairs, though
because Hirohito came on a state visit that November and when
I saw that little Nip coming up the White House steps, my first
instinct was to plug him before he could pull one of them long
swords they all carry, only I remembered Henry's briefing and
it all went off okay, except I naturally never let him get behind
me or between me and the door.

CHAPTER SIX. I GET CAMBODIA STRAIGHTENED OUT
I just got Cambodia straightened out (*see Chapter Two*). They
released the *Mayaguez* in May 1975, not the Fall of 1974.

The Studebaker was a black '69 sedan. You can't just *lose* a
thing like that, in my opinion.

CHAPTER SEVEN· MOSCOW, TEL-AVIV, CAIRO
It was during the winter of 1974-5 that I engaged in my round of
talks with the leaders of the Soviet Union, Israel and Egypt
This was, I think, the first time in the history of the world that a

US President had got so much in in so short a time, it was very like the week Myra and me, Betty and me, spent in Yellowstone National Park when we saw bears, the Mirror Lake, Old Faithful the geyser, climbed nearly three mountains and also got to see *Sands of Iwo Jima* at a drive-in outside Pitchfork, Wyoming. Or it might have been Yosemite National Park.

Boy, could that Studebaker travel! Of course, in them days, it still had its own filler-cap.

Anyhow, these talks I had were of terrific importance to the future of democracy and world peace and the oil and all, so it's only right I should spend a little time here in recording what passed; though, naturally, a hell of a lot of stuff is secret, and I wouldn't put it in a book, you know how people talk about what they read, sometimes it ruins a movie, people sitting behind you going on and on about the damned book it was based on.

Still, some things I am at liberty to divulge. Anwar Sadat, I recall, was very keen to continue the détente, and I go along with that: he and I are currently the two most powerful men in the world, and there are special responsibilities. I did my best to make Leonid Brezhnev see that, but you know Jewish people, I love them very much but they can be damned excitable, look at the way they paint New York green every March 17, and I don't think he was listening too well, and as he has no interest in swimming, it all kind of petered out. Yitzhak Rabin is a great guy, he swims in the Nile every morning, and he gave me his autograph, he is in no way high-hat. All in all, the whole thing was a terrific success, a lot of foreigners in the White House and not even a teaspoon missing when we counted up.

CHAPTER PROBABLY EIGHT: AUSTRIA AND THE MOON
In June 1975, I fell down three times, most notably at Austria Airport in Austria. There has been a lot of comment about this, and I guess I should set the record straight. Well, people forget that a President is a man with a lot on his mind all the time. Other people walk around, they can concentrate on making sure the left leg comes after the right leg, and the relevant arms are getting swung in the proper order etcetera, but it's not so easy for a President. All the time I was doing that walking, I was thinking: *I know I put that goddam blue cap down somewhere*.

In July, I talked to the Apollo-Soyuz link-up. It was a very symbolic occasion, showing how co-operation between two great nations can lead to wonderful understanding. It is my firm belief that relations between us and the Soyans have never, in consequence, been better.

## CHAPTER TEN?: THE SPIRIT OF '76

Between the summer of 1975 and now, much has happened. I won't go into all the details, because it makes the headaches start, but it now looks like I'm going to have to stop being President. I don't feel too sore about that, I have a lot to do, such as looking for the Studebaker and so on, and if the people of America feel that it is time for a change, that is what this great democracy stands for. However, I would just say this: in six months time, it looks as though the United States is going to have to choose between, My God! an old movie star and a guy who builds peanuts. Is this, I ask myself, the sort of destiny the Foundling Fathers had in mind four-score-years-and-ten ago when they fought for independence from the Indians?

I have never tasted Mr Reagan's peanuts or seen any of Mr Carter's movies, but one thing I know for sure: whoever wins, the United States Presidency will not quickly recover its credibility.

# Masters Of Failure

READERS, these are great days for England! I grieve only that I have so long to wait before I can look back upon them with the perspective they deserve . . .

'. . . *wheel me out into the sunshine, nurse, park me over there beside Frobisher. Splendid, thank you. Morning, Frobisher!'*

'*Hallo, Coren, how's the liver?'*

'*Not bad at all, old man, not bad at all. Bit big, but it works a treat.'*

'*They tend to be a bit big, pigs' livers. But roomy. When it comes to new organs, err on the side of roominess is my motto. They put a couple of cats' lungs in me last year, I can't raise my hat without running out of puff.'*

'*I say, Frobisher, do you know what today is?'*

'*Not your ninetieth birthday is it, old man? I'd have sent a card.'*

'*No, no, not for months yet. No, today's the fiftieth anniversary of the sinking of British Leyland!'*

'*NO! Really? By heavens, the old British Leyland, there was a company, went down like a stone with all hands, and every man-jack of 'em singing, I understand. Glorious!'*

'*Wonderful! Magnificent! Still brings a tear to the eye.'*

'*A lump to the throat. Didn't Lord Ryder go down with her?'*

'*Still smiling, I believe, Frobisher. Yes, Stokes and Ryder, the Raglan and Cardigan of their generation! Had the British Woollens Industry not also collapsed without trace, we should no doubt be wearing nice comfy ryders now, old man.'*

'*With stokes sleeves.'*

'*Quite. Do you remember the Great Woollens Industry Disaster, Frobisher?'*

'*Clearly. There were sheepmen weeping in the streets. Wiped out by the foreigners, to a man. Undercut to pieces.'*

'*But their heads were high, eh?'*

'Unbowed, Coren, unbowed! I say, wasn't that just after the old Concorde vanished?'

'It was indeed. What a story that is to tell one's grandchildren!'.

'I do so regularly, old man. How wave after wave of sterling was sent in, millions upon millions, backs to the wall, flags in our hands, theirs not to reason why.'

'While all the world wondered, Frobisher.'

'To give, Coren, and not to count the cost. Remember how the relief column nearly got through to Norton-Villiers-Triumph?'

'It was never on, but what matter? They had to try because . . .'

'. . . because it was there.'

'Exactly! What more need one say? Do you know, Frobisher, I still have a commemorative QE2 ashtray?'

'I'm not surprised at all. They made fifty million. It was probably the biggest melting-down operation in the history of shipping. They say you could see the glow from fifty miles away.'

'Cost me four pounds, Frobisher.'

'Four pounds, Coren! How that takes me back! Do you remember pounds?'

'DO I REMEMBER POUNDS? I was in the City the day the pound fell to three yen! It was the most spectacular currency collapse since the notched stick! They say you could hear the wailing and keening from fifty . . .'

Joys yet to come, friends, tears of nostalgia and pride still unshed! Was ever a race so committed, so devoted, to enshrining and immortalising its failures?

We date our very conception from someone else's successful invasion: the first date in that bizarre diary that logs our weird island story is 55 BC, when the expanding Romans waded ashore and assumed the freehold. We do not even have a *myth* of successful inception, no legendary wolf-teats, no breathy coupling of Olympian gods, no lights in the night-sky calling some son of ur-Britain to found a people or seek a site, nothing.

We get beaten, and we commence.

The first inkling of any such folk-hero does not appear until six centuries later, with King Arthur.

Who is remembered only for his morte, and the fact that his wife ran off with somebody else. Incidentally (though still pursuant to our theme), you may recall that as far as the former feat is concerned, i.e. his death, he promised to return to us. But, on the mere, the wailing having died away, nothing, to my knowledge, has been heard from him since.

Little subsequently happens until the ninth century, when Alfred burns the cakes. As far, that is, as the persistence of his memory is concerned: nothing is popularly recalled of his codifying of the law, his creation of the navy, his invention of the civil service, or what I am told was his highly readable translation of Orosius's *Universal History*, let alone the fact that he actually succeeded in putting the Danes in their place.

All of which makes Alfred the quintessential failure-hero: for, and here is the point, since I do not pretend that no Englishman has ever been a success, *even when an Englishman has succeeded, we have struggled to seek out a failure by which to remember him!*

Take, a scant century later, King Cnut. Not only was he King of England, he was also top man in Denmark and Norway, which he conquered in 1028. After having invaded Scotland, of course, in 1027 and forced King Malcolm to take off his crown and fall to the rush-matting, forelock in hand. Yet who among our pimply pupils, not to mention their parents, remembers him as anything but an elderly twit up to his knees in surf, shouting unsuccessfully at the English Channel? Damn lucky not to have his name worse mis-spelt than Canute, all things considered.

And, hardly had he gone to his ignominious box, than Harold got a crack at the title. A great warrior and magnificent leader, in September 1066 he marched to Stamford Bridge and wiped the floor with a Norwegian invasion force twice the size of his own army. His claim to *fame*, however, rests on the fact that a week later he was unlucky enough to get his eye shot out, thus allowing the Normans to overrun Britain, ruining the natural development of Romanesque architecture and mucking up the Anglo-Saxon language beyond all hope of repair.

Leave us not dwell too long on the unfolding list of British royal failures, William Rufus, shot off his horse while hunting (well, *I* don't recall anything else about him), or Richard I, chiefly remembered for being incarcerated, or John, totally remembered for losing his jewellery in the Wash, for we have other fish to fry; or, at least, to drop on the floor and get covered in sawdust.

For somehow we must get to the bottom of this unique British curiosity, determine the reasons why every year, on November 5, a fortune is spent not only on commemorating a cock-up but also in burning in myriad effigy the man who failed to bring it off. We must fathom the national psyche to find out why we have forgotten all our successful polar explorers in favour of remembering Captain Scott, who not only got to the Pole second, but didn't get back from it at all, to say nothing of Captain Oates, who having failed even more dramatically is the more dramatically remembered. No doubt, had they got there and back again without a scratch, the *Discovery* would now be several nests of Edwardian tables and Captain Scott remembered chiefly as the grandfather of the Severn Wildfowl Trust.

Why, if we stopped the average Englishman in the street and requested that he nominate the three or four most heroic moments in England's history of often quite successful military endeavour, would he immediately reel off The Charge of the Light Brigade, Mons, Gallipoli, Dunkirk, Arnhem, possibly chucking in Trafalgar, but only because Nelson, having been gradually eroded in the course of his career, received the coup de grace at it and is etched on the British memory mainly by virtue (or vice?) of his ambiguous last words?

Name a SINGLE British airship other than the R101.

We don't even have murderers like other people. The most famous killer in British history is Doctor Crippen, entirely because of the spectacular way in which he was caught.

And did we ever have a more popular king than Edward VIII?

Pity that Mallory and Irvine didn't live to see him abdicate, really, but then one could hardly expect Britain's two most famous mountaineers, having disappeared into the mists of Everest's peak, to emerge again.

Quick, what is our most famous and coveted sporting trophy? Absolutely right, it's the Ashes! Now name any other country whose mf & c st is one which commemorates their most abject failure in their national sport, and the winning of which can never be a triumph simply because it merely takes them back to the point at which they should never have lost it in the first place.

And all because of that freaky quirk in our national temperament which maintains that it is somehow improper to win, ill-bred to succeed, that victory is vain-glorious and gallant failure in a worthy cause the most a decent Englishman may strive for. What embarrassment, what blushing hems and haws, the *Titanic* saved us from! How those few brief glimpses of the Brabazon soaring along the ground stirred the post-war soul after the multiple discomfitings of victory! How we . . .

I shall stop there. I feel the argument drawing to a successful conclusion, and I wish to abort this noble attempt before it fouls itself with triumph. I am already growing uneasy about my boastfulness; or, by association, our boastfulness. For it seems we are better at failure than anyone else has ever been; and, glancing from my windows at the currently panic-stricken streets, the country seems poised to enter what may well come to be known as The Golden Age of Failure.

I think we have taken it too far, got too good at it. Too successful. I think we ought to start considering how to fail at failure, at last.

For all sorts of reasons.

# Pro Pecunia Mori

*Until recently, it was not generally known that I had served in Angola with the 17th/21st Boys' Own Mercenaries. It is now.*

*MONDAY*

It is war, and because it is war, it is the waiting that is the worst part. I have been sitting in this rat-infested crater for two days now with my automatic in the mouth of the MPLA corporal opposite, waiting for the CO's cheque to clear. Dear God, what do they know of war at Coutts?

Was it only last Saturday I got him? It seems an eternity since I sprinted through the scrub, bullets zipping past like tin bees, slid down the crater, and there he was, ten quidsworth of NCO.

'I'VE GOT ONE!' I yelled.

The lieutenant crawled up on his belly and looked over the edge.

'Right,' he said, after he'd verified the bloke's shoulder flashes in his *Small Savers Guide To Used Wog Prices,* 'kill him!'

'Hang on,' I said, 'where's the money?'

The lieutenant took out an English fiver, and chucked it into the crater.

'What's this?' I shouted. 'He's not a bleeding private, you know! It's a tenner for corporals.'

'Don't come that, son!' he yelled back. 'Down in Umtasi, B Platoon's knocking off corporals for *four!*'

'You want to get your facts straight,' I said. 'That's *dozens.* Fifty quid a dozen, they round 'em up in trucks and douse 'em in petrol, it's money for old rope. I give discounts for groups as well, I'm not saying I don't. But individual items are a different matter. Look at the work, look at the overheads, and this is no cowboy flame job, remember, he's going to get bullets, could take as many as three, *and* I've been after him all day, costed out he comes to less than a quid an hour. I'd be better off as an au pair.'

The lieutenant took out a little black ledger.

'You charged eight quid for a sergeant last Wednesday,' he said, 'it's all down here.'

'I had a special on sergeants last Wednesday,' I countered, 'eight pounds apiece, or thirty for four. I had this big dayglo sign up outside my hut, just before we burned down Mgoli, GRAND FIRE SALE EVERYTHING MUST GO! You can't use that as an excuse. Tell you what, sir, seeing as it's you, I'll kill him for nine and you can have his teeth. I can't say fairer than that. Even then, I'm cutting my own throat.'

He thought about this.

'Will you take a cheque?' he said. 'We're a bit short at HQ right now.'

'Bloody hell!' I cried. 'Those fat swine at base don't know what it's like up here at the Front! Sitting on their backsides, coining the . . . all right, but make it out to cash and put it on the next runner. And remember, I don't touch this trigger till I see the greenies!'

That was forty-eight hours ago. Those incompetent Blimps at Base could cost us the war. Or at any rate, the profit. A normal forty-eight hours is worth a gross of heads in anyone's book.

*TUESDAY*

Thank God, the relief column got through this morning with the cash, and early enough for me to shoot my bugger's head off and not have the whole day wasted. I rejoined the platoon, and we pushed on to Ebsosa, where the MPLA were rumoured to have set up a field HQ full of top brass, and with colonels at two hundred quid a head, it was an opportunity not to be sneezed at.

Still, it was clearly not going to be all roses. For one thing, I'd been seconded to artillery for this job, and it's four men to a 105 mm, not to mention the terrible effects of HE shells on enemy personnel: frequently you fire at a position held by anything up to ten men, score a direct hit, and when you get there you can only find enough bits to make up half a dozen, and that's if you're lucky. Divvied up four ways, it hardly covers your bar bills, sometimes.

I remember once, when Nobby Clarke and I were on the bazooka, we finished the day with only one leg and a few bits of gristle between us.

'Less than a quid there, old mate,' said Nobby. 'Let's toss for it.'

'Heads!' I called.

It came down tails.

'No hard feelings?' said Nobby.

''Course not, my old son,' I said, and stuck my bayonet through his throat.

He was a good 'un, was old Nob. Fetched thirty-six quid from the other side, once I'd processed him through this middle-man I've got in Luanda.

*WEDNESDAY*

Young Raleigh went to pieces this morning, just outside Ebsosa.

'I thought you were looking after him, Coren!' snapped the lieutenant, with Raleigh just standing there and sobbing like a girl.

'What can I do?' I replied. 'He's just a kid. He was my fag at Borstal. They're sending them to us fresh out of remand home, these days.'

'What's the matter with him?' asked the lieutenant.

'He can't stand killing the women and children,' I explained, 'can you, Raleigh, old chap?'

Raleigh rubbed his sleeve across his eyes, and shook his head.

'You—you only get fifty pee a head,' he sobbed. 'I sp-spent all day yesterday on the bloody m-machine gun and ended up with less than a fiver.' He glared up at us bitterly. 'The lies they tell you in Blighty!' he cried. 'Will I ever get a Jensen now?'

I could not take the disillusion shadowing his reddened eyes. I had to look away, at the bleak scrubland and the wheeling vultures, thinking my own thoughts.

'Will any of us?' I said quietly.

*THURSDAY*

It was a very effective barrage we laid down at Ebsosa last night: £463.70 laid out, as against a return of £2,140.00, after the medics had gone round finishing off the wounded.

We took the town just before noon, which gave us a whole afternoon's daylight for looting and pillaging. The lads always leave the raping till it gets dark, it's easier that way if you can't stand the sight of black women. Not, of course, that I want to suggest that all our blokes are sex-maniacs: most of us are professionals who get all the kicks and satisfaction we need out of killing and maiming, and, come evening, we're usually content to just put our feet up and skin something for a souvenir, while one of us plays *Tipperary* on the mouth-organ.

Tonight, I was standing on the verandah of the ad hoc mess we had set up in what was left of Ebsosa hospital, watching the smoke curl up into the plum-red sky from the pyres which the regimental accountants always light at the end of the day's totting, and generally feeling at peace with the world, when our company commander, Charlie 'Demented Psychopathic Butcher' Helliwell, strolled up the steps.

'Evening, Coren,' he said, 'stand easy.'

'Thank you, sir,' I said.

He smiled.

'This is an informal chinwag, old fruit,' he said. 'Call me Demented Psychopathic Butcher.'

'Thank you, sir, I mean Demented Psychopathic Butcher,' I replied, glad that the darkness covered my blush.

'Coren,' he said, 'I've been meaning to have a word with you. I caught sight of you disembowelling this afternoon, up near the school. It was splendid work. I have decided to recommend you for a commission.'

'I say!' I cried.

'Just 2% to start with,' he went on, 'but if you make captain, and I have every reason to believe you will, there'll be an extra 5% over and above, of course, your normal rate, plus the bonus for massacre.'

'I don't know what to say, Demented Psychopathic Butcher,' I murmured.

'No more than you deserve, old chap,' he said.

The men were in a more sombre mood when they woke up this morning. We were supposed to advance on the railhead at Ingisi, and word was that it was being held by Cubans; and possibly Russians, too.

Conscious of my new responsibility as a commissioned officer, I stood up at breakfast.

'Look, chaps,' I said, 'I know what a lot of you are thinking. Just remember that a Russian soldier isn't much different from your barefoot wog with his pointed stick. He's just better trained, better disciplined, and better armed, that's all. If you see any, run like hell.'

They cheered up a bit, after that, and, pausing only to blow up what remained of the town, we moved out. So quickly did we make time, in fact, that by lunch-time, we found ourselves a mere ten miles from Inglisi. Demented Psychopathic Butcher's armoured jeep roared alongside my platoon, slewed to a halt, and my commander dismounted.

'Right!' he shouted. 'For once, Base Intelligence was on the ball, Inglisi's full of your Marxist scum! Given their fire power and experience and all, we're going to have to pull out all the stops! I've come up with a whole new strategy!'

'Oh, well done, sir!' I cried.

'Yes,' he said, 'all of us officers will crouch behind this rock. The white NCOs will crouch over us, covering us completely, and the white Other Ranks will crouch over *them*. Then we send in our crack black battalions. After that, we'll tot up and see where we stand.'

'But we might end up earning nothing!' cried young Raleigh.

The CO stared at him savagely.

'Forgive the lad, sir!' I intervened. 'It's just that he hasn't had the edges rubbed off his idealism yet. He doesn't know what it's all about.'

Demented Psychopathic Butcher shrugged at last, turned on his heel, and threw himself beneath the rock. We followed, in strict order of superiority. We waited.

I do not know how long we crouched there, in our own darkness. All I know is that when we eventually unfolded, it was all over. Our blacks lay dead, in a trim row, and, a few yards off, so did theirs. Through my field-glasses, I could see a Russian officer totting up on his pocket calculator. The CO looked at me.

'This could get a bit nasty,' he said, 'if we don't play our cards right.'

I knew what I had to do. I stood up. I dropped my weapons, noisily. I walked across to the Russian. I took out my cigarettes.

'Papeerosa?' I offered.

'Pazhalsta!' he replied, taking one.

We smoked for a while. After a minute or so, I made up my mind. I nodded towards our officers. He looked. He shrugged. He nodded towards his, crouching under their own rock. I looked. I shrugged.

We shook hands. I walked back, and so did he.

'What did he say?' asked the CO nervously.

'It'll be all right,' I said. 'You know, sir, these chaps are just like us, really.'

The CO nodded.

'Funny thing, war,' he said.

# Morality Play

'According to The General Household Survey just published by Her Majesty's Stationery Office, Everyman 1975 is a figure dissatisfied with his job, struggling to buy a house, a car, and a telephone, and beset by guilt over his inability to give up smoking' – Daily Telegraph

## Characters

| | |
|---|---|
| EVERYMAN | GRAFT |
| CONFUSION | CORRUPTION |
| MOTOR INDUSTRY | GUILT |
| POST OFFICE | MORTGAGE |

DEATH

## EVERYMAN 75

Here beginneth a treatise how the High Father of Heaven sendeth Death to summon every creature to come and give account of their lives in this world, and is in manner of a moral play.

*( Semi-detatched premises  A hallway. Enter EVERYMAN  His tie is under his ear. There is a livid umbrella-ferrule wound on his left cheek  His hat is dented. His shoe has trodden in something. Paperwork is falling through a hole in his briefcase.)*

EVERYMAN            What is it all for? I embarked upon my journey at 5.37 and it is now 6.49. I descended at Chancery Lane in orderly fashion and a ticket collector would not change my pound note. 'What do you think I am, the bleeding Bank of England?' he screamed at me, indicating a notice requesting correct change wherever possible. I informed him that my correct change had fallen through a hole in my pocket brought about by reduced circumstances, i.e. wife going out to work due to mortgage increase also penal rate rises, and was now rolling around inside my coat-lining . . .

(*Enter Confusion*)

CONFUSION   Why is your wife rolling around inside your coat-lining?

EVERYMAN   Not my wife, my correct change.

(*Exit Confusion, stepping on cat*)

EVERYMAN   . . . and he said 'Step aside and wait', and I did, and a whole mob of people suddenly went mad, there was this sound of an incoming train, you see, and they swept over me, and bent my denture. So I missed my connection at Baker Street for Finchley Road to connect with the Rickmansworth train, and while I waited I put 5p in the chocolate machine and when I pushed the drawer back in after the peanuts came out and broke all over the platform, it caught my tie in it.

(*Enter Confusion*)

CONFUSION   What peanuts? When you pull the chocolate drawer, it is supposed to produce winegums. Will you write to the company, demanding your 5p back and compensation for your tie?

EVERYMAN   Yes.

CONFUSION   Good, they've moved to Exmouth. By the time your letter catches up with them they'll be out of business.

(*Exit Confusion, blowing fuses*)

EVERYMAN   If only I had a car! I should drive to Rickmansworth every night, and to Holborn every morning! I would listen to the push-button transistorised radio, and watch the cigar-lighter pop out, and flash my headlamps at AA men, I should arrive refreshed as a result of the specially body-contoured neo-rexinette seating plus unique headrest, my face cooled by the infinitely adjustable airflow system!

(*Enter Motor Industry*)

MOTOR INDUSTRY    Here's a lucky thing, here's a lucky thing! Got just the model, new on the market. the Yakimoto Loganberry 1300 in tasteful two-tone heliotrope, genuine wind-down windows and Sukiyaki radials all round, special introductory offer only £987!

EVERYMAN    Why, I think I might just be able to afford, I mean, let me do a quick calculation on the back of this . . .

MOTOR INDUSTRY    No rush, squire, give me a ring.

(*Exit Motor Industry, over geraniums*)

EVERYMAN    Wait! I haven't a telephone, I mean I'm waiting for them to . . .

(*Enter Post Office*)

POST OFFICE    Everyman, Everyman. let's see, no Everyman on this list, sure you're not the British Home Stores, Lewisham?

(*Enter Confusion*)

CONFUSION    No, he's not, as a matter of fact he's Belwether & Fungus Ltd.

EVERYMAN    No, I'm not, it's just that I keep getting their letters, we have a similar address, according to the Post Office, that's how the trouble arises, they're at 14 Pondicherry Crescent, Dundee, and I'm at 73 Gladstone Road, Rickmansworth, you wouldn't believe the time I spend re-addressing their . . .

POST OFFICE    Werl, it's a natural mistake, can't blame the Post Office, honestly, some people, we're up to here in wossname, not to mention the Italian dock strike, inflation, and snow on the points at Haslemere,

|               | what about these snails in your letter-box, then? |
| EVERYMAN      | Snails, what snails, I thought you'd come about the telephone I ordered in 1972? |
| POST OFFICE   | Ahem! |
| EVERYMAN      | What? |
| POST OFFICE   | Ahem! AHEM! |
|               | *(Enter Graft and Corruption)* |
| GRAFT         | Drop him a fiver! |
| CORRUPTION    | A tenner! |
| TOGETHER      | Twenty! |
| EVERYMAN      | I haven't got it, there's the mortgage, the insurance, the rates, the children, the food, the cat, the gas, the electricity, the HP, the fares, the tax, the . . . |
|               | *(Enter Guilt)* |
| GUILT         | Give up smoking! Put it away, a fiver a week, think of your lungs! |
| EVERYMAN      | You're right! I will, I must! |

*(Exeunt)*

## SCENE II. ONE MONTH LATER

*(Enter Everyman. He is green, haggard, trembling. He sucks Polos endlessly.)*

| EVERYMAN | They shout at me, they all shout at me, why do they shout at me? I have dedicated myself to selling annuities when I could have been throwing bridges across the Orinoco, lying at night beneath the stars in the arms of a big-busted mulatto, I could have been in Tahiti painting Polynesian girls with bums like plums, I could have been discovering the North-West Passage in the company of randy Eskimo triplets, but instead I have given my youth to selling annuities and still Mr Wetherall shouts at me and his secretary sneers and loses my chitties! If I had a detached property, a Yakimoto Logan-berry, a white bedside telephone . . . |

|  |  |
|---|---|
| | (*recovers*) What am I saying, I have saved my twenty pounds, the telephone is as good as mine, I . . . |
| | (*Enter Post Office*) |
| POST OFFICE | Ahem! |
| EVERYMAN | Yes, right away, here's the . . . (*Enter Mortgage*) |
| MORTGAGE | I'll take that! (*Snatches note*) |
| EVERYMAN | WHAT? You're taken care of, standing orders, regular payments, ten per cent interest . . . |
| MORTGAGE | *Eleven* per cent, now, if you don't mind! Twelve by next week, with a bit of luck. We must take account of inflation, reflation, depression, recession, the sliding, the floating, the crawling, the falling . . . |
| POST OFFICE | Not to mention snow on the points at Haslemere. |
| MORTGAGE | Not to mention snow on the points at Haslemere. |
| POST OFFICE | Werl, that's it, then. (*Exit*) |
| EVERYMAN | But if I don't have a phone, I can't order a car, and if I don't have a car, I can't get respect from my colleagues, if I can't get respect from my colleagues, I can't hope for job satisfaction, if I . . . |
| | (*Enter Motor Industry*) |
| MOTOR INDUSTRY | Good evening, good evening, good evening! I was just passing, just back from delivering a new Rover 2000, automatic, fully-reclining front seats, power-steering, to your Mr Wetherall, just passing, thought I'd drop in! |
| EVERYMAN | Hurrah! No need to phone you! I have not touched my nest-egg of £987, rather have I given up smoking at great personal distress, please supply one two-tone heliotrope Yakimoto Loganberry 1300 as per our order of the fifteenth ult! |

| | |
|---|---|
| MOTOR INDUSTRY | You must be joking! Everybody knows the Yakimoto Longanberry 1300 has just gone up to £1,264.53, excluding seat-belts, of course. |
| EVERYMAN | Oh God, oh God! (*Bangs head on sideboard, froths, stops, clenches fists, looks up with new determination.*) Never mind, all is not lost, I shall take my £987 and purchase some secondhand model in v.g.c., 20,000 mls. only, 1 prev. own., outstndg bgn.<br>(*Enter Confusion*) |
| CONFUSION | About the £987, it appears that the solid, gilt-edged, blue-chip company in which you invested the said sum has just gone up the Swanee. |
| EVERYMAN | AAAAARGH!<br>(*Exeunt Mortgage, Motor Industry, and Confusion, sniggering severally*) |
| EVERYMAN | A cigarette, a little cigarette, a little friend, a little cigarette to lean on, what care I for job and family and roof and Loganberry and STD when I have my little friends, where are you, little friends (*begins tearing open cupboards frantically*), I know you're here somewhere, come out, come out, wherever you are! (*Rips drawer from sideboard, finds packet, pulls out yellowed cigarette, and, lighting up, inhales deeply.*) Oh, that's good, that's so GOOD!<br>(*Enter Death*) |
| DEATH | 73 Gladstone Road, Rickmansworth? |
| EVERYMAN | That's right. Who are you? |
| DEATH | *Who am I?* Who do I bleeding look like? How many people go round with empty eye-sockets, wearing a black shroud and carrying a scythe? |
| EVERYMAN | Are you an advert for something? Should we have a packet of it in the house? Could I win a glorious sun-soaked holiday for two in fabulous Benidorm? |

| | |
|---|---|
| DEATH | Ho yes, I should bleeding cocoa! I'm Death, mate, that's who I am, aren't I? Death. |
| EVERYMAN | NO! Really? That's terrific, that's wonderful, you couldn't have come at a better time, I've never been so pleased to see anyone in my, er, life! |
| DEATH | Pardon? You do know why I'm here? You're scheduled to pop your clogs, mate. Kick the bucket. Snuff it, conk out, pass over. |
| EVERYMAN | I know, I KNOW! Isn't it marvellous? No more bloody annuities, no more mortgages, no more guilt or confusion or failure or derision! When do we start? |
| DEATH | You meet some funny buggers in this job, I don't mind saying. All right, Belwether, get your coat. |
| EVERYMAN | Who? |
| DEATH | Don't muck me about, son, it's been a long day! Are you or are you not Julian Belwether of Belwether & Fungus Ltd.? |
| EVERYMAN | No. I'm Everyman. They're at 14 Pondicherry Crescent, Dundee. |
| DEATH | That'll be bloody Confusion, putting his oar in! Doesn't it make you sick? I'll be off, then. |
| EVERYMAN | Off? What do you mean, off? You can't leave me like this, can't I volunteer, where do I sign, when can we leave? |
| DEATH | Do give over, son! If you're not Julian Belwether, you're not bloody coming, and that's that. You wouldn't believe the paperwork. You could be another thirty years yet, we're up to our necks in Accounts. *(Exit Death)* |
| EVERYMAN | Thirty years? Thirty *years*? *(He falls to his knees. He breaks down. He weeps.)* |
| | **CURTAIN** |

# And The Living Is What?

AT LAST, now that the thunder of the guns has echoed away over the battlefield of the Liberal Party, now that the groans of the wounded and the cheers of the victors alike have faded, we political commentators can stand back and what's that the cat's dragging across the lawn?

Sorry about this.

I shall be back with the future of the Liberals in two shakes of a

The thing is, with temperatures in the nineties, it behoves each and every one of us in this great country of ours to take a particularly close look at what our cats are dragging about; with the rate of rotting up around Mach 2, today's dead chaffinch is tomorrow's epidemic. Walk past our dustbins, giant bluebottles whang up like grouse; in the small hours, you can hear them knocking the lids off.

It's a large goldfish. Or was. The cat freezes, paw on gill, glares up with a feral eye; a tiny Douanier Rousseau tableau, rife with threat. Is the strange heat reverting the moggy to type? Are old genetic echoes running through its system? Are its little DNA molecules ricocheting about like hot popcorn, filling it with jungly urges?

I pull it off the fish. The cat, I swear, growls. It watches, with its new malevolence, as I pick up the goldfish. The tail is dry, the colour ebbs from it as I watch; weird, like the last frame of *Dorian Gray* when the young face ages fifty years in death.

Just before I re-address myself to the Liberal future, I ought to decide what to do about this little corpse. Where did the cat get it? Are neighbours even now gazing into their reft ponds and penning notes to stick on gates? *Goldfish, may or may not answer to name Charlie, missing from 32* . . . What should the caring citizen do? Go round from door to door with the last mortal remains on a plate, probing ex-ownership? *Good evening, you don't know me, I'm from Number 26, I was just wondering . . .*

No. Best to dispose of it. Can't leave it for cat to eat, can't tell what might happen to cat if it tastes fresh, well almost fresh, meat, next thing you know it could be dragging elderly relatives off to its basket.

Dig small hole behind greenhouse, drop goldfish in it, pat down earth, wash, return to typewriter.

For David Steel, I have nothing but

You may wonder what I'm doing writing in the garden; and, the fauna having interrupted the easy flow of political argument, you have the right to an explanation.

I normally type at the top of the house, a roomlet under the eaves, a romantic snug carved from the living joist; most nights I'm locked there like some mutant heir in a Victorian melodrama. But it is a spot that collects all the spare heat in the house, and squares it, prising open every pore of the hapless saunee and offering the wet fingers the chance to type lines like 'Ay ladt, moe thar tje yhunfer of yhe gubs gas exhord asta . . .' which as openings of political articles go, has little on its side but mystery. Not only that: up there, the heat has driven the very fabric of the building crazy—the roof creaks like a wind-jammer, the tank gurgles, the tiles gnaw one another, pipes burp.

So I carried the machine down into the garden. A hot afternoon, but a light breeze in spasms, some shade under the tree, a jug of coolant beside the Olivetti, the whole thing not unlike the urban writer's dream of a bee-loud tax haven somewhere beyond the International Date Line, a spot where the bones thaw and warm tranquillity nourishes the images, do a novel a week in a place like this. Once you've buried the fish.

Glad I explained that.

Now, then.

For David Steel, I have nothing but the greatest oh Christ a bee has fallen in the jug. Big bee, like an angry muff. Not much gin in it, mainly tonic, but how much gin does a bee need before it reckons it can lick anyone in the place? Nevertheless, we are all part of the great chain of being, we must love one another or die, if man does not help bee, what does the future hold for any of us?

Got nothing to get bee out with. Roll up piece of paper, bee ignores it, hydroplanes madly around the surface of the booze like a blob of phosphorus, bouncing off ice cubes. It is getting angrier, it does not see the foolscap as a lifeline, but a weapon, it is doubtless pumping all its venom towards its armoured bum ready for its kamikaze blast, girding itself to die with name of queen on lips.

Lips?

Finally—does it appreciate the sacrifice?—I tip the jug out, the Gordons sinks into the brown grass, the bee plods about in its little alcoholic swamp, grounded. I have no plans to dry it out, I have gone as far in charity as I am prepared to go, I leave the bee to sort itself out and go for a fresh jug.

When I get back, with a good sentence held carefully in my head about John Pardoe, the liquid patch is alive with starlings, doubtless as dry and thirsty as the rest of us. They clatter up as I approach.

They have eaten the bee.

At least, the bee is no longer there, and as it could not have had time either to dry out or sober up, we must assume it is now working its way down some airborne gizzard.

If I'd left it in the jug, it could have passed quietly from this vale of tears in utter painlessness and woken up across The Great Divide with the last verse of *Nellie Dean* still murmuring from its smile.

I am not ready for nature and its imponderable ways. I ought to be up in that airless room.

For David Steel, I have nothing but there is water falling on the paper.

I look up, there is the impenetrable foliage of the acacia. Rain will not fall through that. Rain, in fact, will not fall anywhere, since there has not been a cloud over these premises for three weeks.

Anyway, the rain is horizontal, which explains why it is now falling on one side of my body only. I look round; there is a rainbow between me and the fence.

It is the work of a moment to rip the paper from the typewriter, scream, and dash round to the neighbour's. A tiny Filipino opens the door, all smiles, a beam on little legs.

'I'm awfully sorry, I wonder if you could possibly move your sprinkler to the other side of the garden, just for a while?'

The smile widens.

'Sprimbler?'

'The water. It's falling on me. If you could just . . .'

She beckons me in, bows me backwards to the kitchen, gives me a glass, points to the tap, smiles even wider.

'Wodder,' she offers generously. 'Wodder for hot. Very hot.'

I drink a glass of wodder, we bow to one another, I walk back, the refilled jug is full of flies, water is running through the typewriter, my notes on the pad beside it are sodden, illegible, like a love-letter to a distant soldier.

I move the table and the chair out of the pouring shade, into the sun, the typewriter dries, I put in a fresh sheet, sweat springs from the skin, I type:

Ay ladt, moe thar tje yhunfer of yhe gubs

I get up, with considerable care and self-control, and go inside with the jug of flies, and empty it down the sink, and turn to the refrigerator, and discover that I did not close the refrigerator door on my last visit so that not only is there no ice but also the floor of the refrigerator is awash with molten butter; a couple of lolly-sticks float across it, lazily, propelled by the vibrations of the machine as, heartbreakingly, it struggles against the odds to perform the function it was put on this earth to do.

Mop up butter, drink warm beer, plod back to typewriter.

Sun hammers down, gnats wheel, brain gums, importance of Liberal Party struggles to make itself felt, no propositions come, no theses surface, just two-dimensional faces, Freud and Henry, the Dowager Grimond, a man who came to the door once, years ago, covered in rosettes, and tried to explain the Liberal stance on Cambodia, or was it Cyprus?

It is some time later when I open my eyes from a dream of pain. The sun is considerably lower, but I do not notice this at once, since all I can see are the figures 6, 7, 8, & 9, in soft focus, these being a millimetre from my left eye, the rest of the face buried in the keyboard. I raise my head, the bunched keys fall back from the platen, my lips are a solid Velcro weld, my entire skin from chin to crown is shrunk, taut, singing with irradiation; I squint down my nose, it is giving off a purpurean shimmer, it is a miracle of metamorphosis, the sun has turned me into W. C. Fields even as I slept.

The table, the MS, the beer-can, are alive with earwigs. Thus Gulliver must have felt. The earwigs, this being the summer of the Giant Crawly—we have greenfly the size of damsons, ants like Dinkies—are huge, French-polished: if they tried to climb into your ear, they'd wedge, you'd have to call the Fire Brigade to pull them out.

Enough. The dream of deft quills whorling beneath Tahitian palms is over; I recall, too late, that Polynesian literature has not, in fact, made much of a mark on the world's bookshelves. I heft the typewriter up, creep inside, the house is cool.

The house is burgled.

There are scattered drawers everywhere, empty cufflink-boxes, open wallets, piles of clothes with gutted pockets, rejected loot strewn insultingly from room to room, cupboard doors hanging open; perhaps a hundred socks, here and there. I sprint through the place, clutching the typewriter still, as if it were a weapon: what shall I do if I corner him? Threaten to type out a meticulous description?

He is long gone.

Two coppers come, shirtsleeve order, trannies nattering. There is much professional peering.

'Yes, well, heatwave, windows open, what do you expect, lot of it about, up the drainpipe, turn it over, down the drainpipe. It's all down to the sun, right?'

'Villains' holiday,' says the second.

'But I was right there in the garden,' I protest.

'People in the garden, what can you expect?' says the first. 'It's the heat.'

'There you are then,' says the second.

There you are then.

97

# A Little Learning

*According to the* Daily Telegraph, *'headmasters today are giving their bad teachers glowing references in order to get rid of them'. Fine; but where, then, are they all ending up?*

MR J. D. HOBLEY, the Senior French Master, strode into the Staff Room, slammed the door, and sniffed disgustedly. The airless premises reeked thickly of dust, chalk, and stale gin. Mr J. D. Hobley stabbed a brown-stained forefinger at the Staff Room Monitor, a gangling fifth-form boy standing meekly by the tea-urn.

'Oy, vous,' he snapped, 'ouvrez la porte!'

Dutifully, the lad ambled across to the door, and opened it.

Mr J. D. Hobley smacked his head.

'Don't get bloody funny with me, son!' he shouted.

He opened the window.

'Want anything done in this place,' he said, 'you have to do it yourself. It's not a profession any more.'

The boy ran snivelling from the room, whereupon the Deputy Headmaster wheeled on his Cuban heel and glowered at the Senior French Master.

'Thank *you* very much!' he cried. 'Me and him was going to *Bambi* tonight. He'll have one of his headaches now, I shouldn't wonder. He's a very sensitive child.'

'Oh, pardonnez-bleeding-moi, I'm sure!' said Mr J. D. Hobley. 'I thought you was knocking about with the caretaker these days.'

Dr Edwin Stokes, a squat, tweeded mathematician sunk deep in a battered fauteuil, glanced up over his bulldog pipe.

'If you're talking about my Kevin,' he muttered, 'I'll thank you to keep a civil tongue in your head. Especially,' and here he raised his voice, 'as it ill behoves certain people to comment on other people's behaviour when certain people owe other certain people 39 pee.'

Mr J. D. Hobley looked at him.

'How d'you make that out?' he asked.

'Gave you a pound yesterday,' replied Dr Edwin Stokes, 'to get me an ounce of Gold Block over the Cat & Wardrobe, didn't I? 77 pee, ounce of Gold Block.'

The Senior French Master took out a pocketful of change, and laid 23 pence on the arm of the mathematician's chair.

'What's this?' said Dr Edwin Stokes. 'Where's the other 16 pee?'

'Wasn't it T. S. Eliot,' murmured a pale elderly man in a wine-spattered linen jacket, 'who said *Neither a lender nor a borrower be*?'

'You tell us,' snapped Mr J. D. Hobley, who was in fact somewhat relieved to have the subject changed, since Dr Edwin Stokes had now taken off his socks and was calculating furiously, 'you're supposed to be Head of English.'

'Our greatest novelist,' said the Head of English, quietly, 'after Shaw.'

'Why did he say it?'

The Head of English shrugged.

'Why does any of us say anything?' he replied, 'I think that's a question for our colleague from the Philosophy Department, not for I.'

'No good looking at me,' said Mr Beesley of Philosophy, through a Jaffa cake, 'I'm new in Philosophy, I haven't got it sorted out yet, it's a whole different wossname, world.'

'Ah,' said the Head of English. 'What did you do in your last job, then?'

'Nothing much,' said Mr Beesley. 'I used to take the dinner money.'

'Why did you leave?'

'They caught me doing it,' explained Mr Beesley. He swallowed the last of his biscuit. 'So it was either a nasty scandal with the law coming in and everything, or else a new job at a new school, so I told the Headmaster right-o, I'll have a go at philosophy.'

'A wise choice,' said Mr J. D. Hobley. 'At least it's in bloody English. *And* you don't have to cart a mob of kids round Calais every year.'

'*Calais?*' cried a small swarthy man by the window. 'Why on earth are you taking them to Calais? I'd have thought that was a job for the Russian Department.'

'What?' said Mr J. D. Hobley. 'Are you sure?'

The small swarthy man sniffed.

'You don't teach bloody geography for thirty years,' he said, 'without picking up certain things. If I had a map, I could probably show you.'

'There's a globe there,' offered the Head of English, pointing.

The small swarthy man snorted.

'Globe?' he sneered. '*Globe?* Another bloody loonie, are you? Another one who thinks the sea wouldn't drip off?'

There was a short laugh from behind the urn. They looked towards it, to see a fresh-faced young physicist shaking his head.

'Not *that* old chestnut!' he said. He stirred his tea carefully. 'Has none of you ever heard of the law of levity? Goodness me, do you not recall the story of the young Isaac Walton standing by the fallen apple tree and saying *Father, I cannot tell a lie, it fell on my head?*'

'All right,' snapped the geographer, 'all right, listen to him. All I know is, you're bloody near the edge at Calais. If you come back ten kids short, don't say you weren't told. It's probably full of kids, underneath. You probably can't move down there for bones in bloody blazers.'

'You ought to take 'em to Tangier,' said Mr Beesley. 'Eleventh school I was at, I took a mixed party to Tangier one Easter, got a tenner apiece for girls in reasonable nick, twenty for a boy, and I'm talking about twelve years ago now. Thirty kids today, you could come home with a new Cortina.'

A bald man beside him nodded vigorously.

'You're so right, Gordon!' he cried. 'I'm an economist, and even I don't understand what's happened. Am I utterly wrong, or are prices going up and up?'

'They are indeed!' exclaimed a spindly lady, who taught botany. 'I can remember when you could have a nice day out in Margate, buy a new umbrella, get an abortion, and still have enough change left for a pound of mushrooms. I sometimes wonder if the H-bomb doesn't have something to do with it.'

'I agree,' said the Head of Physics. 'There's some sort of

conspiracy here, unless I'm very much mistaken. Do you notice how they never tell you what the H stands for?'

'Government!' thundered Mr G. Rumbold, Acting Head of History. 'If you ask me, we were all better off when we had a Tsar on the throne.'

'It's all there in the Bible,' said the Rev. P. Holbein. He tapped the palm-stained book on the desk beside him. 'There is nothing that has not been said before, nothing that . . .'

Mr Beesley, who was perched on the edge of the desk, flicked the book open. 'His rough brewer's finger ran thrillingly along her marble thigh,' he read.

The Rev. P. Holbein snatched the book from him.

'A stupid error!' he cried. 'I took that filth away from a misguided third-former just the other month!'

Whereupon he hurled it across the room into a wastebasket. Mr J. D. Hobley walked over and fished it out. He smoothed the creases carefully.

'Twenty quid a dozen these cost me,' he said, 'and that's just for printing. Never mind sitting up at the bloody typewriter night after night.'

The spindly botany lady cleared her throat.

'Oh dear!' she said. 'I do wish the Head would come!'

The others nodded, and fell silent. There was no sound save the low gargling of Matron's still. The young chemist looked round, puzzled.

'Sorry,' he said, 'but what's this about? Where *is* the Head?'

They looked at him.

'Haven't you heard?' asked Dr Edwin Stokes. 'He's interviewing Moira Gill of 5b. Terrible girl, incorrigible, absolutely frightful business.'

'I trust the Head will be firm,' said the Head of English, 'for everyone's sake. I've told him we support him absolutely.'

'Quite,' said Mr G. Rumbold. 'If the Head doesn't put his foot down, I fear the worst for the dear old school.'

They sighed, in their thoughts, but snapped alert at a sudden footstep. The doorknob turned; the door opened.

The Head's round face was oddly grey. His eyes looked down.

'I'm afraid,' he said, 'that I'm going to have to marry her.'

# Bottle Party

*'Boozers are being offered the bender of a lifetime: an alcoholiday in the sun. The special attraction is twelve hours' drinking a day, FREE! Tourists will pay £45 for the trip to the island of Majorca, and for their money they will get unlimited supplies of liquor at a three-star hotel. Tours manager Colin Woolf said: "Our clients will be able to drink until they fall down."' —*Daily Mirror

**Hotel Borrachera**
**Playa de Palma**
**Majorca**

*38th July* 1977

DEAR AUNTIE THING, Alice, tall woman, big yellow teeth,

Well, here we are at the, oops, there's a blotty, hallo Blotty! Who's a pretty Blotty then? at the, you know, and we are all having a wonderful O God Almighty these bloody Spanish pens! THESE BLOODY SPANISH PENS! THESE STINKING BLOODY LONG-HAIRED GREASY SPANISH WOG CHEAP LOUSY ROTTEN

Expen the scusil. Thrown pen over balcony, whee goes pen, hope it sticks in Spanish head, ha-ha, serve them right throwing Norman out of El Wizzo Niteclub just because Norman sick on bongo, no business having bongo where people can be sick on it anyhow, how they expect Norman do Knees Up Mother Thing with six bottles of vino sloshing about in him?

Norman lucky didn't get run over, all mad drivers, also hate dogs, don't realise thing running out of El Wizzo on all fours is man doing brilliant impression of airedale, Norman now got tyre marks all over his nice El Wizzo tablecloth.

And what police doing banging on hotel door in small hours, anyone think it crime to borrow tablecloth, no business grabbing Norman either, man got perfect right to be on top of own wardrobe, paid for room didn't he? Only reasonable Norman lash out with Genuine Old Master showing Majorca at sunset. Man was desperate. As I informed magistrate, 'We did not splash three quid on priceless antique work of art just to have rotten fascist pig stick greasy head through it.'

Norman back now, got lice. Also had to share cell overnight with violent criminal, quantity surveyor from Wimbledon staying at posh place in Palma on fourteen-day gin excursion, went mad when barman tried to close bar, bit barman's ear off. Disgusting putting my Norman in with him, Norman never ate anyone in his life.

Glad I brought up food.

Oh God.

Here I am, Auntie, back again! Where was I, oh yes, glad I mentioned food, food quite good, really, except too much paiella, trouble with paiella is you get shrimps in hair when face falls in it after third bottle, steak days are best except when they overcook it and you bruise your cheek.

Went to see fullbight last Monday where is my cigarette and sat in the sun with these gourds Norman bought where you have to squirt the wine into I KNOW I PUT MY BLOODY CIGARETTE DOWN SOMEWHERE where you have to squirt the wine into your mouth, only after the first couple of gourds Norman squirted it into ear of woman sitting next to him, woman scream blue murders, Norman leap up, woman's husband leap up, sock Norman in his O JESUS AUNTIE PILLOW IS ON FIRE PILLOW IS BURNING, AUNTIE, AUNTIE, I MEAN NORMAN, NORMAN, PILLOW IS ON FIRE NORMAN.

O GOD AUNTIE NORMAN IS ASLEEP ON LOO WITH SOMBRERO ON MUST CLOSE NOW BACK LATER.

Back now, Auntie, it nearly dark, whole place smelling of foam. Not my fault, threw burning pillow off balcony, woman on balcony below leaning out drying hair in breeze, pillow land on head, hair flare up like chip-pan, woman shriek, people upstairs smell burning, call fire-brigade, fire-brigade come, no hydrant so attach pump to swimming pool supply, drain swimming-pool dry and find two English couples lying on bottom surrounded by bottles, police doctor say they dead two days. Funny thing, Norman wondered why conger line shorter than usual at El Wizzo last two nights.

Meanwhile man downstairs put wife's head out with fire-extinguisher, woman now not only burned bald but face all wrinkled up from chemicals and suntan fallen off, woman look like old golf ball. Husband ran upstairs, kicked in door, punched Norman in face, Norman fell off loo, now asleep in bath, so everything a bit calmer now.

Poor Norman, got black eye now to go with cauliflower ear received at bullfight after husband of woman with wine in ear sock Norman in his. Terrible blow, after that Norman see four bullfighters sticking four swords into four bulls every time he look.

Everybody know only two bulls and two bullfighters, clear as nose on thing. Two noses.

Anyway, Auntie, after bullfight met very nice English couple lying underneath charabanc, grocer from Birkenhead and lovely wife Arthur. All went out for dinner together, and Arthur danced in soup.

Arranged to meet on beach next day, and great fun burying Norman, falling down in sea, throwing ice cream at boring Swede families, etcetera, until it was time for lunch. Invited couple back to our hotel for five or six bottles. Only when half-way through second course and Arthur asleep on butter dish that Birkenhead grocer suddenly start counting.

'What is it?' I ask him.

'What is two and one?' he reply.

We think for a bit.

'Three,' I say finally.

'Thought so,' he comment. 'We never dug up Norman.'

Rush back to beach, dragging Arthur by foot, Arthur's arms flailing about knocking things off tables as we cross dining-room, bloody lucky most diners asleep under tables, but one or two Germans, French, etcetera start kicking up fuss when chicken legs start falling in laps, screaming, shouting, terrrible thing about foreigners, can't hold their drink.

O GOD AUNTIE I AM SOBERING UP. IF NORMAN COMES ROUND AND FINDS ME HE WILL GO SPARE, HOLIDAY COSTING HIM FORTUNE HE SAYS, MUST DRINK TWELVE BOTTLES

A DAY JUST TO BREAK EVEN, WHERE TELEPHONE, WHERE ROOM SERVICE?

Hallo Mummie, Auntie, fat old cow, fancy giving us a wooden toast rack for a wedding present NO I DON'T BLEEDING FORGET EVEN IF IT IS TWELVE YEARS YOU FLY-BLOWN OLD RATBAG, feel a lot better now, nice bog bittle inside me, good idea having spiders walking all over the wallpaper, keep the flies off, especially green spiders, hallo green spiders wherever you are, I hope your troubles are few, all my good wishes go with you tonight, I was a spider, too, hee-hee-hee-hee-hee, O TOOTH ALMIGHTY I HAVE BROKEN A GOD ON THE BEDSIDE TABLE

hallo norman

Norman did not want me to wake him up Auntie he has hit me with the bidet HOW DID YOU GET THE BIDET OFF THE WALL AUNTIE, NORMAN, BELOVED, HOW DID YOU MANAGE TO why are my slippers floating past?

I have to close now Auntie, the manager has ordered a car to take us to the airport YES I AM REFERRING TO YOU YOU SWARTHY DAGO PIG I WOULDN'T STAY ANOTHER MINUTE IN YOUR BUG-RIDDEN RAT-HOLE FOR ALL THE TEA IN IN IN I DON'T KNOW WHERE SO STICK THAT UP YOUR CASTANET AND FLAP IT HAR HAR HAR.

You know what it is, Auntie, don't you, you know what it is all right, you know what it is with these bloody people, they're just a load of filthy anti-British bigots, that's what it is!

Hoping this finds you as it as it as it thing,
Your loving niece,

er,

# And A Happy Saturnalia To All Our Readers!

THE MAGI eased themselves down from their horses, wincing, and blew on their fingers. They had had a cold coming of it. Not to mention a cold going back.

Melchior took the myrrh out of his saddlebag and stared at it.

'We aren't half going to cop out,' said Gaspar gloomily.

'He'll go up the bloody wall,' he muttered. 'I bet we won't even get expenses.'

'I've a good mind to hang on to the gold,' said Balthazar. 'We could say we got mugged. We could say prices in Bethlehem have gone right through the roof.'

'He'd never wear that,' said Gaspar. 'He'd have our hands off at the wrist before you could say Jack Robinson. Heads up on poles as well, I shouldn't wonder.'

'Come off it!' cried Melchior. 'We three kings of Orient are!'

'*Were*, more like,' said Gaspar. 'Be lucky to end up as we three corporals.'

They shuffled wretchedly inside, and knocked on a door marked MAGUS-IN-CHIEF.

'Come.'

They went in. The Chief Magus looked at them. He saw the still-wrapped gifts.

'What's this, then?' he said, slowly.

'Couldn't find Him, could we?' replied Balthazar.

'You *what?*'

'Solid cloud,' said Melchior. 'Couldn't see a hand in front of your face, never mind stars. We asked all over, though.'

'It was like looking for a needle in a wossname,' said Gaspar. 'It's got more stables than you've had hot dinners, Bethlehem.'

The Chief Magus glared at them for a long time.

'You realise what this means, I suppose?' he muttered. 'It means no Christmas, that's what it means! It means bloody Saturnalia again, orgies, sacrifices, people off work for a month, production up the spout. And what about this lot then?'

He pointed to a pile of paper in his out-tray.

'What are they?' asked Melchior.

'Christmas cards,' snapped the Chief Magus. 'Only spent the last three days writing addresses, didn't I?'

'You'll have to nail some ads up,' said Gaspar, 'telling people you're not sending cards this year.'

'Or any year,' muttered the Chief Magus bitterly . . .

The Chairman stood on the opposite pavement of Oxford Street and stared across at his store. Above the giant papier-mâché models on the façade, a banner shrieked MERRY SATURNALIA 1976! in great, red, sateen loops.

'You'll notice,' murmured the Head of Design, indicating his creation with a lily hand, 'that this year's leitmotif is rape.'

'It always is,' said the Chairman.

The Head of Design glowered at him through burning lashes.

'I happen to be very into tradition,' he said tightly., '*Some* people think it's very hip to have a load of symbolic perspex tat about the birth of the sun, but I'd rather be *dead* than oblique. I suppose you fancy Harrods' rubbish this year, all dancing rhizomes with funny hats on and Mother Nature in a garlic G-string?'

'I didn't say so,' said the Chairman.

'You didn't have to, Dennis. I could see it in your face. It was one of your Looks, wasn't it? Personally, I think it's sickeningly twee. I mean, it might be all right for *their* market, lot of sentimental old dykes coming up from Cheltenham to buy French reproduction telephones, but it isn't ours, duckie. We're at the solid, no-nonsense, family end of the market, people coming to us want to see something they can understand.'

'I suppose you're right,' said the Chairman. He shielded his eyes against the sharp December sun. 'What exactly *is* that that Uncle Holly is doing under the sled?'

The Head of Design sighed, rolling his eyes.

'The trouble with you, Dennis,' he said, 'is you don't get out enough.'

The agent shook his head doubtfully.

'I'm not happy about this,' he said. 'I'm not happy about this at all. Couldn't you just rough him up a little? Knock a few teeth out, break his arm?'

'Out of the question,' said the Head of Light Entertainment. 'The BBC Saturnalia Variety Spectacular is the high point of the year. With an £18 licence-fee, the public has a right to a decent human sacrifice. What kind of a finale would it be if the Vestal Virgins just danced down the stairs and knocked the star's teeth out? There's going to be twenty million people tuned in on Boxing Night, just had a nice dinner, full of booze and seasonal spirit, how are they going to feel if after all that, if after sitting through the obscene ventriloquists and Schumann's Lascivious Horses and Royal bloody Ballet excerpts from *Nude Lake,* they're forced to watch Des O'Connor just crawl away in splints?'

'But *decapitation*!' protested the agent. 'Des has always been such a snappy dresser. What's he going to look like with his head off and his lavender tuxedo ruined?'

'He can count himself lucky,' said the Head of Light Entertainment. 'London Weekend are going to boil Reg Varney in oil.'

The agent sighed, and drew the contract towards him.

'Go careful at rehearsal,' he said, scribbling his name. 'Remember, I got a family to feed.'

Arthur Sidgewort hung the last rhino-horn on the tree, wound up the satyr on the top, and climbed down the step-ladder.

'I suppose I'll have to sleep with your cousin from Stockport again,' he said.

'Maureen's very nice,' said his wife, adjusting a fairy-light so its gleam fell across a dangling rat. 'She always brings something for Grandpa.'

'Last thing she brought was that inflatable brunette,' muttered Sidgewort. 'Her stopper flew off in the middle of the night and she whizzed round the room smashing all the souvenirs he brought back from Spion Kop.'

'She's never said an unkind word about you in her life,' snapped his wife. 'She likes you very much.'

'You don't have to tell *me* that,' said Sidgewort. 'Last Saturnalia, I didn't get out of traction till February 3rd. I suppose it'll be you and my Uncle Norman. I don't know what you see in him.'

'I don't see anything in him, Arthur. That's the whole point. Saturnalia is a time for giving. Sometimes I don't think you know the meaning of the word charity.'

He was still glowering at her when the doorbell rang. He opened it. There were two dustmen standing on the mat, beaming and touching their caps.

'Merry Saturnalia, squire!' they cried.

Arthur Sidgewort turned his head.

'Doris,' he called, 'it's for you!'


In the vestry of Mars-by-the-Wall, Bromley, the Rev. J. D. Huggett took off his laurel wreath, sighed, and pulled on his rubber coxcomb.

'I think the moth's been at the skin, vicar,' said his sexton, shaking the fleshtint folds and struggling with the zip. 'Perhaps we ought to get a new Father Saturnalia outfit for next year.'

'Don't be ridiculous, Mimsey!' snapped the Rev. J. D. Huggett. 'Where's the money coming from? If there was anything in the kitty, would I be going out in this filthy sleet to sing carols for the caryatid fund?'

He stepped into the legs of the skin and worked it up over his body.

'We've put on a little avoirdupoids since last year, I do believe!' simpered Mimsey. 'I think I'll put a stitch in that navel, it's stretched something terrible.'

The vicar pulled up the zip, not without difficulty, and tugged at the nipples to bring them into some sort of reasonable symmetry.

'How do I look?' he said.

'Not *terribly* nude,' said Mimsey. 'I think it's the leather elbows.'

'It'll be all right in the dark,' said the vicar. 'I'll look naked from a distance. The boys can stand on the mat, I'll sing from the gates. How is the choir dressed this year?'

'They're broad beans,' said the sexton. 'I thought it'd make a change from radishes.'

'Good thinking, Mimsey!' said the vicar, nodding his comb, and stepped out into the inclement night.

The twelve broad beans fell in behind his plump figure, acceptably pink in the streetlighting, and the little procession moved out of the graveyard, walking in single, relatively dignified, file until they reached the first house.

Whereupon Mimsey advanced up the path with the collection box, the Rev. J. D. Huggett twanged his tuning-fork against a convenient gnome, and the broad beans opened their little mouths and in a clear, sweet soprano began to sing:

'Four-and-twenty virgins came down from Inverness, and when the ball was over there were four-and-twenty less, singing . . .'

# Plus Ça Change

*In which I preview another wonderful crop of French books for 1978.*

CETTE FOIS A BEZIERS

In this shattering new tour de force by Marguerite Duras, a man (called, with reverberative simplicity, M. Homme) arrives in Beziers one morning, or thinks he does. He may actually be in Laroque-des-Arcs. He takes a room in a small hotel, whose one window overlooks the rear entrance of a discount tyre warehouse. He does not notice this at first: the opening four chapters concern the way in which he is staring at the bedside table, until, in the seminal Chapter III (which reappears as Chapter XXVII), he throws his raincoat at it. In Chapter V, he leaves the room for the first time and goes to the lavatory at the end of the corridor. Arriving there soon after the opening of Chapter X, he looks at a crack in the washbasin, returning to his room in Chapter XIV in order to compare the crack in the washbasin with a button that has fallen off his coat. 'Could all this happen in Beziers?' is what Homme asks himself. It is then that he walks to the window and sees some old tyres in the yard opposite, and realises for the first time that the road is 8.76 metres wide, not including pavements.

This is a wonderful book which says everything it has to say with an assured disregard for purpose. For 704 pages I was kept wondering: why am I reading this? And it is a measure of Mlle Duras's commitment that it was a question which remained implacable at its own answerlessness.

POMPON ARRACHE SON NEZ

As a change from the resonant austerities of Duras, I turned to this delightful Gascon romp in which the inhabitants of a small village, incensed at the discovery that the Chief of Police has a talking pig, eat their mayor. Discovering what has happened, their priest, the lovable cross-eyed, one-legged, stone-deaf, half-mad Senegalese dwarf (a beautifully delicate piece of character-drawing, this), decides that as a punishment, the Angel of the Lord should come down and turn that year's unprecedentedly marvellous vintage into vinegar. He accordingly prays for this miracle, and, sure enough, a seven-foot tinker with a vulture perched on his head walks into the church. Believing him to be the Angel of the Lord, the priest falls to his knees and explains what he wants done; but, to the priest's considerable chagrin, the tinker turns out to be the editor of a communist newspaper who is in love with the daughter of the major wine-grower of the area, and who has come to the village in disguise to woo the girl against the wishes of her Poujadist father. To unfold further the brilliant plot would be to ruin this wonderfully warm and human story of life in provincial France, so let me just say that M. Chasserieu has once again excelled himself with a portrait of rural manners and mores second to none.

### L'HISTOIRE D'U

U is a very rich young aristocratic girl who lives in a ninety-four-roomed apartment overlooking the Bois de Boulogne. Every morning she goes out onto her balcony, with nothing on beneath her rubber poncho, to watch the horses pass; whenever one of them breaks into a gallop, U falls down in a faint, frothing at the mouth, and scraping her fingernails along the harsh gravel of the balcony, a noise which itself drives her six maids wild with Sapphic lust and ensures that none of the silver is cleaned for at least two hours thereafter.

A big black doctor is called by U's stepfather, the Duc, and the doctor, having humiliated the patient with a number of spatulas and ophthalmoscopes, informs her father that she is repressing her urge to be a mare. Distraught, the Duc enquires as to possible lines of therapy, and the the doctor suggests that U be entered in the forthcoming Prix des Folles at Longchamps. As the Duc is a prominent racehorse owner, this presents fewer problems than might at first appear, the Duc's major worry being that he already has a horse, Mignonne, entered for the race, and may not be able to get a ranking jockey up on his daughter in time, unless he switches riders, which he is loth to do, since Mignonne has a good chance of winning.

In the event, he finds an apprentice, Alphonse Pinaud, who is willing to ride anything just for the experience of taking part in a big race. U gets a flyer out of the starting-gate and is lying second at the first bend when she suddenly catches sight of a particularly fetching stallion about to pass her on the inside. Mad with passion, she careers headlong into the rails, throwing Pinaud and breaking several ribs with a pain that drives her into delirious ecstasy. Waking up in Belleville Hospital, she finds herself purged of hippophilia, and rapes her osteopath.

A brave, challenging, and extremely dirty book, *L'Histoire d'U* richly deserves its place in the pantheon of Modern French literature. It will be thumbed and thumbed.

INNOCENTS, TOUS
Turning from fiction, we come to a major piece of painstaking historical research in which M. Gustav Pontfilet at last proves conclusively that nobody in Occupied France ever saw a German, let alone spoke to one. M. Pontfilet, who worked for the French underground during the war and received the Croix de Fer for the impeccable efficiency with which he kept the platform of Réamur-Sebastopol free of inferior races, has interviewed over twenty thousand Frenchmen who did not collaborate with the Germans, more than thirty thousand who never heard of anyone who collaborated with the Germans, and forty thousand more who thought the war ended in May 1940 and had never been able to understand why Ernest Hemingway had carried a gun when he burst into the Ritz bar in 1945 and always assumed it was because some *crime passionel* was taking place on an upper floor in which he had a marginal interest.

Lavishly illustrated with photographs taken at the time in innumerable towns and villages, all of them showing Germans nowhere to be seen, and with invaluable graphs demonstrating how trade in Paris and along the Riviera fell by almost one per cent during this dark period, *Innocents, Tous* explodes the myth of Franco-German co-operation and nails this foul canard once and for all.

## THIS FOUL CANARD

Taking as his starting point the moment when he was served, at the famed Restaurant des Mamelons Risibles, an absolutely foul canard which he promptly nailed to the wall, Oscar Pasdequoi takes us on a picaresque tour of the grand disasters which it has been his sad duty as a Guide Michelin inspector to suffer: a truffled frog-bladder in Nîmes that defeated four of France's leading gastro-enterologists, a piece of gravel in a stuffed wren that resulted in his swallowing a tooth which subsequently ruptured his large intestine; a large intestine *à la manière de la Vicomtesse de Bragalonne* which proved to have been a small intestine inflated with a bicycle pump before being brought to the table and which therefore exploded when the flaming calvados was poured over it, resulting in the loss of M. Pasdequoi's hearing and a million pound lawsuit; and a crab at Le Crétin which woke during consumption and clamped its remaining claw on M. Pasdequoi's lip where it remained throughout Easter (since his doctor had decamped to Juan-les-Pins with Madame Pasdequoi, who had grown sick of her husband's refusal to grant her a rosette for the meals she prepared at home and had finally cracked when he wrote to her complaining of sloppy service).

Certainly, of the 1,131 books on cuisine so far published this spring, *Canard* bids fair to be the one most likely to engender the sort of thrilling controversy on which French literature depends for its very life. Already, one Prix Goncourt judge has been maimed by a fish-kettle, and two respected sommeliers have jumped from the Eiffel Tower, locked in one another's arms.

## BONJOUR VIEILLESSE

Let us welcome another exhilarating new novel from the adroit pen of Mlle Françoise Sagan. In this one, a shy young virgin of 49 falls for a married man many years her senior, enraptured by his maturity and his style (he can take out his teeth, reverse the plates, and reinsert them without his hands ever leaving the rims of his bathchair), overwhelmed by his sophistication (in a whirlwind tour of Europe, they visit twelve spas in seven days), thrilled by his love-making (his elegant Louis XV bedroom has pulleys everywhere), and stunned by his wealth (he made his first fortune by the time he was thirty by taking bets on the outcome of Verdun), she turns her back on her own generation of swinging St Tropez knitters and becomes his bride. But trouble is , of course, in store when her husband's only son returns from prostate surgery and sets eyes on his ravishing young step-mother for the first time. . .

Another winner, another gem in the bright diadem of modern French letters! Ah, would that the sluggish pens of other races but follow where these virtuosi lead!

# We hAve AlaN cOreN
## iS TherE Any aDvaNcE ON 4 ovid?

THE EAR may be a dust trap, but when it comes to keeping your sunglasses on, it has clear advantages over a drawing-pin pressed into the side of your head.

These days, we must concern ourselves over such details.

Similarly, there are many places for a forefinger, and a matchbox isn't one of them. Decimalisation is tricky enough, without our having to convert imperial pints on an arsenal of only nine digits.

Anyone currently awash in my drift has clearly not been reading the newspapers: kidnapping, it seems, has much in common with rabies in that, having swept the European mainland in the last few years, it now stands poised at Calais waiting for a good following wind, and if Something Is Not Done the people of Britain may well, in the days to come, find themselves spending more and more time in car-boots, tea-chests, cellars and attics while loved ones scurry back and forth in frantic attempts to drum up something negotiable to wrap in brown paper and leave in a hollow tree off the A41.

I give you, courtesy of the *Daily Express,* Mr Peter Heims, editor of *Top Security.* As if it weren't disturbing enough to think that there's enough interest in the subject to merit a magazine called *Top Security,* its editor has a tale to make thy two eyes, like stars, start from their spheres: for he is presently gumming together a seminar at a Heathrow hotel to discuss ways in which potential British kidnapees can keep the stocking-mask from the door, and those invited include such top retailers as

116

Marcus Seiff, John Sainsbury and Sir John Cohen (which just goes to prove that there is a darker side to turning over umpteen million jars of jam than lying on one's yacht and totting up the week's gross), plus *fifteen hundred* others, like Richard Burton, who have made no secret of the fact that they have no need to duck into a doorway when they spot their bank-manager strolling towards them.

Addressing this throng of collateral will be a team of experts including Sir Geoffrey Jackson, our erstwhile ambassador in Uraguay, who was recently nicked by Tupamaros, and who avers: 'We must bring home to people that kidnapping can happen here and that it's got to be stopped. It is important to step up on manpower and firepower in making it infernally difficult to be captured.' He then, having got the blood racing and Messrs. Smith and Wesson excitedly scribbling quick calculations on the back of an old cartridge-box, adds an even more disquieting coda: 'But if terrorists really want to get you, believe me they will.'

And it is that small phrase which sends the brain spinning into crazed speculation: 'if terrorists really want to get you.' For how does one determine *that?* Fathom the convoluted, possibly illogical, workings of the terroristic psyche? Might they want to get *me*? Or would it be mere money up the spout to bung an electrified fence around the premises, mount a Bofors gun on the roof, chain myself to the boiler, and invest in a matched pair of Dobermanns of such keyed-up suspiciousness that they would be as likely to start stropping their fangs on the master's shins as go for the putative kidnapper?

On the surface, yes. The tie that binds such unlikely bedfellows as Mr Burton and Sir John Cohen is their common ability to spill noughts on a cheque without a second thought, and needless to say I am not of their number. The number I am of is £137.63, at the last count, and I'm not altogether certain it didn't have a red 'O' against it, come to think; and one of the few things I feel entitled to guess about kidnappers is that they do not go to all the trouble of grabbing a customer only to find themselves with an overdraft to pay off. One's first thought, indeed, is that it's rather comforting to know (since I haven't been invited to attend) that there are fifteen hundred blokes standing between oneself and the Elastoplast gag, and that British kidnapping will have to become something of a craze before the threat gets around to me.

One's second thought, however, is that the said fifteen hundred would be pretty dumb to stand up and be counted, that what Mr Heims has probably got on his hands is a vast empty auditorium with Sir Geoffrey Jackson staring down at it, and that Britain's would-be kidnappers are back to square one, i.e. pot luck.

So what? you say. Even if they're not going to be ticked off that Heathrow guest-list, there are still large stocks of millionaires around, all of them better quarry than a bloke with nothing more than £137.63 of someone else's money. True enough; but there's scant consolation there, because a quite unsettling aspect intervenes in the argument at this point.

As you doubtless know, Italy is so beset with kidnappings these days that it is virtually impossible to drive through Rome or Milan for the vast traffic-jams of plain vans containing solvent citizens trussed like chickens. As a result of this, rich men have taken to dissembling: they drive battered old Fiats, wear crumpled off-the-peg suits, sport tin watches, smoke dog-ends, and, more ominous than any of this, actually pay a new breed of PR men to spread the word in the public prints that they are on their uppers and do not know where their next lira is coming from. It's reaching the point where, unless these terrified lads are very lucky indeed, they will be snatched *for looking so broke they could only be loaded!*

It is therefore open season on everybody. And, if Sir Geoffrey's any judge, the same could happen here: merely by drawing attention to my overdraft I ensure that kidnappers immediately assume me to be drowning in the stuff. Ah, you say, but when they find out, they'll let you go!

Yes, I reply, and probably in slices.

Then again (and here we wade into yet murkier depths), though I may personally be broke, that is not to say there are not people on whom my kidnappers might lean, assuming *them* to have the wherewithal to repurchase me. So I have to begin asking all sorts of questions I would prefer to leave unframed, e.g. how much would *Punch* pay to get me back? A thousand? Fifty thousand? Anything? True, there might be some goodwill to be gleaned from forking out a few bob to save a loyal colleague, but Wm. Wordsworth is not the only hack to hear Two Voices: I hear another saying, with maximum TV coverage, 'Much as we love Mr Coren, we feel that a stand must be taken NOW if the country is not to be overtaken by a wave of similar atrocities. Let us stand up to these thugs! Let them see that we would rather sacrifice one man than put a thousand in jeopardy! This magazine has always stood for law and order, for decency and courage, for an Englishman's right to walk the streets without fear, for rattling good value at only 25p and although in this week's bumper issue there is no article by Mr Coren, there are nevertheless pages and pages of wonderful hilarious . . .'

The kidnappers might send the note to my wife, of course, and I've no doubt she could scrape a few bob together, here and there, under the circumstances, and certainly would. Almost certainly would. It has just occurred to me that due to the quirk of fate that men call insurance policies, I am worth a considerable amount of negotiable tender, dead. Normally, this would not weigh at all with this warm and devoted girl; but let us just suppose that I was snatched on a day upon which we had been bunging saucepans at one another and

She would, of course, change her mind when the heat died down, but by then, if I happen to fall into impatient hands, I could well be anchored in the Estuary by a pair of concrete socks and moving only with the assistance of the tide

I am not sure what to do for the best. Like most of us, I have up until now reckoned my redemption to be in hands about which I could do nothing. Human beings, I fear, are fallible redeemers. I suppose the only course is to remove the uneasy options from them, and see to it that one isn't nicked in the first place.

I intend to have THIS BELONGS TO THE MAFIA tattooed on my chest. It may be painful, but it'll hurt less than having an ear removed at the root, and will almost certainly prevent it.

Provided, that is, I get a kidnapper who can read.

# Face Value

*'We didn't think to ask whether Mr. Cheeseman really was a US colonel or a South African spy or anything. In a small village, you just take people for what they are'* – Interviewee on BBC News

THE BELL JANGLED above the green-glassed door of the Village Store. The shopkeeper glanced up over his bi-focals, and inclined his head deferentially.

'Good morning, Your Holiness,' he said, 'what can I do for you?'

'Twenty Embassy,' said the Pope, 'and a box of Smarties for the wife.' He took off his cap, rolled it up, wiped his nose with it, unrolled it, and put it back on again. 'Bleeding parky this morning,' he said.

The shopkeeper swung the brown paper bag between thumbs and forefingers.

'Well, you'd notice it after Rome,' he said. 'Personally, I don't find it too bad for May. I can see where you wouldn't want to be out on no balconies waving, of course. It's probably why Catholicism's never really caught on in England.'

'You put your finger on it there, all right,' said the Pope. 'Even in Rome, I never do any of your *alfresco* blessing during the winter. Wind blows straight off the Baltic, goes right through you, you'd catch your death. What do I owe you?'

'Fifty-three pee,' said the shopkeeper.

'Ah,' said the Pope. 'Couldn't put it on the slate, could you? I've only got lire on me, I come straight off the plane.'

The shopkeeper sucked his teeth, opened a tea-stained ledger, removed a pencil-stub from behind his ear and ran its point down the columns.

120

'That makes it £14.33 this month, Your Holiness,' he said. 'You couldn't see your way clear to, er . . .'

'Friday,' said the Pope. 'Soon as I get my envelope.'

The shopkeeper shut the ledger.

'You must get sick of the journey,' he said, 'week in, week out.'

'You wouldn't chuckle,' said the Pope, nodding. 'Not to mention the bloody airline food. I said to them last week, I said, not bloody egg mayonnaise again, I said, here I am spiritual leader of five hundred million people, you'd think I'd get a hot dinner now and again.'

'Beats me why you don't move,' said the shopkeeper. 'Don't tell me they couldn't find you a nice little flat near the Vatican.'

'It's not that,' said the Pope. 'I'd miss the whippet.'

'You could take him. You got a nice big square out front, I've seen it in pictures, he could run round that.'

The Pope shook his head.

'Full of tourists,' he said. 'People see the Pope running round after a whippet, it could knock the bottom out of the souvenir business for good.'

'I never realised,' said the shopkeeper.

'Not your job,' said the Pope. 'See you.'

The door banged behind him.

It opened again.

'Nearly forgot,' he said, 'pax vobiscum.'

'Ta,' said the shopkeeper.

The door banged shut again.

The shopkeeper's wife came up from the cellar, bearing crates.

'Who was that?' she enquired.

'The Pope', said her husband.

'How's Doreen's sciatica?'

'Forgot to ask.'

'Beats me how she puts up with him,' said his wife, filling a shelf with beancans from the crate. 'He never takes her to Rome. I never thought she'd come back after she ran off that time with Rex Harrison.'

'Rex Harrison? I never knew she ran off with Rex Harrison! He was in here yesterday enquiring about the Maxwell House Free Kitchen Knife Offer which should have been attached to the 8oz jar he bought on Tuesday. I told him it must've blown off. He never said anything about running off with the Pope's wife.'

'Oh, it was years ago, he's probably forgotten. He'd come back briefly from Hollywood, I remember, to see if that cellular underwear he'd ordered had arrived yet. Next day he took Doreen off to Clacton in his private jet. I wouldn't have known myself, except I saw ex-King Zog of Albania down the launderette, he was full of it, well, you know what he was like, it's not surprising they abdicated him.'

'That and his impersonations,' said the shopkeeper, nodding. 'They must have got sick and tired of him going round Albania in a fez and saying "Just like that" all the time. No wonder the Communists took over.'

'That reminds me,' murmured his wife, 'you know Alexander Solzhenitsyn?'

'I ought to,' he said, 'it was his youngest gave Kevin impetigo up the Juniors. What's he after now?'

She handed him a scrap of paper.

'He gave it to the boy this morning,' she said. 'He's cancelling *Dalton's Weekly* and *The Sun*. He expects someone to pedal all the way up there just to deliver *Melody Maker* once a week, it's not on, is it?'

'Here!' said the shopkeeper, jabbing his finger at the note. 'He's spelt *Weekly* with an *a*. My God, Beryl, the people they give Nobel Prizes to these days, I don't know what it's all coming to!'

'He's probably all right in Russian.'

'Clever bloody dick, he was just the same when we were in the Cubs together. Ordinary knots weren't good enough for him. Well, he can come down here and collect the bloody paper himself, customer like that, hasn't bought a quarter of dolly mixtures all the time he's been back here.'

The bell jangled again. They looked up.

It was a small elderly man in a herring-bone overcoat and gumboots. 'Good morning,' he said.

'Good morning,' said the shopkeeper.

'I've just moved in,' said the little old man. 'I've bought Shrew Cottage.'

'Oh,' said the shopkeeper, coldly, 'so you're Frank Sinatra. I didn't recognise you without the wig. Well, our books are filled. No more tick customers. Good morning.'

'Hang on,' said Frank Sinatra, 'my money's as good as anybody else's. I just met Adolf Hitler down the ironmonger, what's he got that I haven't?'

'He's a gentleman, that's what,' said the shopkeeper's wife. 'He doesn't put his hands all over you. He may have had a bit of a chequered past, forcing people to live on dried egg and put black paint on their headlights and everything, but he's never preyed on women to my certain knowledge. Have you ever known Mr Hitler do dirty things, Wilfred?'

'Never. I'd trust my own sister up Dunconquerin.' He took his glasses off. 'Singers is something else. There won't be a woman safe.'

'I've packed up the singing,' said Frank Sinatra. 'I'm living off a nest-egg I've got in the Leek & Westbourne. Women don't go for small investors, you know, especially without wigs.'

The shopkeeper sucked his teeth.

'I dunno. What do you think, Beryl?'

'You don't wear after-shave or anything?' said Beryl.

Frank Sinatra shook his head.

'Nothing like that at all,' he said, 'unless you count Steradent.'

She sighed, shrugged. 'I suppose it's all right,' she said.

Frank Sinatra thanked them, touched his hat, went out.

The shopkeeper looked at his wife fondly.

'You still know how to temper justice with mercy, Beryl,' he said. 'You haven't lost your touch.'

'You never do,' said his wife. 'Not when you're born to it. It's like riding a bicycle.'

Her husband put his arm around her shoulders.

'The country will never know what it lost, Beryl,' he said.

'Oh, I don't know. That woman from the agency is doing all right. It beats me how she stands it, opening factories all the time, driving around foreign parts in terrible heat, going on horses. I could never stand horses, it's one of the reasons I jacked it in while I was still a kid.'

'I always thought it was because you didn't want to marry a Greek,' said her husband.

'There was that, too,' she said.

# My Tent's In The Highlands

*News that rich Arabs are buying up Scottish land and castles and moving in could not have come at a better time for Scottish poetry . . .*

TO A CAMEL
Gret, reekin, moldie, mangie beastie,
O, welcome tae oor humble feastie!
Who wad hae thought ye quite so tastie,
                                    Wi' neeps and tatties?
Come, set we doon and gobble hastie
                                    Oor camel patties!

SHAIKH LOCH-IN-VAR
O, Shaikh Loch-in-Var is come out of the East,
Through all the wide Border, his steeds are the best!
A puce Lamborghini, a carmine Ferrar-
i, plus two yellow Rollses, drives Shaikh Loch-in-Var!

He roars through the Highlands at over the ton,
Pursued in her Alfa by Wife Number One,
Who's followed by Wives Two, Three, Four, in *their* cars!
Was there ever a harem like Shaikh Loch-in-Var's?

Behind speeds their eunuch (who really quite likes
The sensation you get on the big motor bikes!)
His thighs grip the flanks of his white Yamaha,
As he screams in the wake of young Shaikh Loch-in-Var!

As they watch him whizz past, the pedestrian Scots
Dream their own dreams of concubines, Bentleys, and yachts;
And they shout at the flash of his bright djellibah;
'Just ye wait till we've got our *own* oil, Loch-in-Var!'


## TO A SHEEP'S EYE
Fair fa' your honest sonsie face,
Great chieftain o' the organ race!
Aboon them a' ye tak your place,
                    Ear, nose and throat!
Weel are ye worthy o' a grace
                    As lang's my coat!


## SHAIKHS, WHA HAE
Shaikhs, wha hae wi' Faisal bled,
Shaikhs Yamani's aften led,
Welcome tae your oily bed,
                    Or tae victorie!

Noo's the day, and noo's the hour!
Charge yon BP drilling-tower!
Sod the Minister o' Power!
                    Hoots monopolie!


## THE TWA CORBIES
As I was walking all alane,
I heard twa corbies[1] making a mane:
The tane unto the tither did say,
'Where sall we gang and sell this day?'

'In behint yon auld fail[2] brake
I wot there sits an oil-rich shaikh;
And naebody kens that he lies there
But his wazir, his goat, and his ladies fayre.'


[1]Corbies=estate agents   [2]fail=turf

'Why!' quoth tither, 'here's luck, the noo!
We'll sell him a brool[3] and a fustie[4], too!
A diggle[5] and aye a comlie crake[6]!
He'll nae ken the difference, yon wogglie shaikh!'

[3]brool=derelict farmland  [4]fustie=fake castle  [5]diggle=mountain
[6]crake=island with no planning permission

# That Old Black Magic Has Me In Its Spell

*'More financial support for the arts from commercial companies is expected to follow the BBC's decision to lift its ban on giving publicity to sponsors of artistic events which it broadcasts. In future, sponsors of these events will be named, and may even be allowed visual acknowledgement in television programmes'* – Daily Telegraph

'NATURALLY,' said the Marketing Manager, 'we wouldn't interfere with the text. Not a word.'

'Not,' said the Advertising Manager, 'a syllable.'

'On their children's life,' said the Chairman.

'On our children's life,' said the Advertising Manager.

'Thank you,' said the head of Drama. 'I think we can all respect one another's integrity, gentlemen.'

The Chairman of Wundatrash Sundries Ltd eased himself from the white hide armchair (brought in palmier BBC days) and walked to the window. He looked down into the cobbled well of the Television Centre, at what had once been the manicured emerald inlays of grass, but were now brown and clovered. The fountains had been cut off.

'This *Hamlet* is a prestige show,' he explained.

'I know,' said the head of Drama.

'Put a foot wrong,' said the Chairman, 'we could end up with a warehouse full of Danish cutlery. At the top end of the market – I'm talking about £18.95 per place setting – you can't browbeat people. Subtle, is what we're after.'

'I understand,' said the Head of Drama. 'Merely a mention at the end of the closing credits, perhaps, to the effect that this production was brought to you by courtesy of Wundatrash Sundries?'

'Makers,' said the Marketing Manager, 'of fine Danish tableware.'

'Plus,' added the Advertising Manager, 'a wide range of

prestige household commodities at a price to suit every purse.'

The Chairman examined the end of his Romeo y Julieta.

'You don't want it,' he said, '*too* subtle.'

In the theatre, the stage lights went up. Francisco and Bernardo, in their rehearsal clothes, met upon the battlements of Elsinore. On each black brick of the crenellated ramparts, a yellow Dayglo letter had been painted. Together, they spelt WUNDATRASH SUNDRIES.

'Dear God!' breathed the Head of Drama, in the darkened stalls.

The play's director leaned across the aisle.

'Do you know what costumes cost today?' he muttered 'Have you any idea how much you have to pay to get Telly Savalas?'

'Who?' said the Head of Drama. 'I understood it was to be Ian Holm.'

'In the sticks,' said a voice behind them, 'who knows from Ian Holm?'

The Head of Drama turned. All he could see was the glow of an orange disc.

'But *Telly Savalas?*' he hissed.

'Very big,' said the disc. 'With housewives, you can't imagine. The name alone has been calculated to shift—' the Chairman snapped his fingers.

'Eighteen ton of confectionery,' said the Marketing Manager.

'—eighteen ton of confectionery,' finished the Chairman.

'I didn't know you made confectionery,' said the Head of Drama.

'A whole new area,' said the Chairman.

The Head of Drama turned back to the play's director.

'Are you happy,' he said, 'with an entirely bald Hamlet?'

The Director did not look at him.

'As you know,' he replied, in a somewhat tight voice, 'Hamlet worries a lot. It is quite within the bounds of possibility that this would have made his hair fall out. Also, I hope to bring out the essential clash between his age and his immaturity. Hamlet is both an adult, thrust suddenly into an adult situation, and a child, a son, Gertrude's little boy, totally unequipped to deal with adult responsibilities.'

'How exactly, since Mr Savalas is pushing fifty,' said the Head of Drama, 'do you intend to present this contrast?'

The director cleared his throat.

'A lot of the time,' he said, 'he will be sucking a lollipop.'


The first act closed.

'Is that it?' asked the Chairman. 'He doesn't marry the girl?'

'They won't like that,' said the Marketing Manager, 'in South-West Sales Division. It's a very middle class area. Also, we were hoping to shift a lot of trousseau stuff, candlewick bedspreads, percolators, matching tablecloth and napkin sets, that sort of thing. You need a bridal scene for that kind of marketing mood.'

The Director sighed.

'There are four more acts,' he said.

'Do me a favour,' said the Chairman, 'we've been here forty minutes already That's half as long again as *Crossroads*.'

'This is, of course, the uncut text,' said the Director. 'It is normal to shape *Hamlet* a little. Here and there.'

'I'm very glad to hear it,' said the Chairman. 'First off, the Ghost goes.'

'The Ghost,' cried the Director, 'is central to the plot!'

'It is also,' said the Chairman, 'central to the Company logo. It walks along that platform under the thing—'

'Battlements,' cut in the Advertising Manager.

'—under the battlements, it's right in front of our name. I wouldn't mind if you could see through it. What kind of a Ghost you got, you can't even see through it? How come you can always see through them in films?'

'It's a photographic trick,' explained the Head of Drama, quietly. 'The actor himself is not transparent.'

'You're telling me!' snapped the Chairman. 'I've been in wholesale a long time, sonny, and what I'm telling you is that we have been looking at a very uncommercial Ghost.'

'I'm just, you know, running this up the flagpole to see if anybody salutes it,' said the Advertising Manager, 'but can't we reach some sort of compromise here, men? How would it be if the Ghost had something on his sheet?'

'What sort of something?' whispered the Director.

'Well – I'm only spitballing – how about DOUBLE-BED SIZE

ONLY £8.95 THE PAIR FROM WUNDATRASH?'

There was a long silence

'Out of the question,' muttered the Director at last.

The Chairman lit another cigar

'Either that,' he said between puffs, 'or no Ghost '

The silence returned. Polonius and Reynaldo stared out at the dark auditorium, awaiting the cue to start Act Two. The Director continued to chew his upper lip. At last, he cupped his hands, and, somewhat strangulated, called: 'Would someone bring me a sheet and a paintbrush, please?'

The Chairman sat back in his seat again. He took out his cigar and examined it

'There's just one thing still bothers me,' he said to the Advertising Manager.

'What's that, BW?'

'You didn't mention the matching pillowcases.'


The Marketing Manager woke his Chairman up as Act Five opened.

'What? What happened?' said the Chairman hoarsely, rubbing his eyes with a vicuna cuff 'Did I miss the wedding?'

'I don't know how to tell you this, BW,' said the Marketing Manager, 'but the girl croaked.'

'*Croaked?*'

'Worse,' said the Advertising Manager, 'she killed herself!'

The Chairman closed his eyes

'Next thing you'll tell me, she did it with a carving knife,' he groaned, 'threatening our entire range of almost stainless budget kitchenware in the special Ophelia Bridal Gift Pack '

'Nearly as bad,' said the Marketing Manager 'She drowned herself in a pool '

The Chairman sat up, leaned forward, and took the Director's forearm in his trembling fist.

'We have twelve gross pre-cast kidney-shaped polystyrene items with mock mosaic surrounds plus genuine plywood springboard to shift, £600 not including installation, and you let her *drown* herself?' he roared.

'Please, not now,' begged the Director, 'this is the graveyard scene!

'The *what?*' cried the Chairman. He wheeled round. 'Didn't

anyone tell him we sold the stonemason's yard?'

'It could be, like, okay,' said the Marketing Manager. 'He says there's clowns in this bit. It could be very up-beat. They're digging with Wundatrash shovels, you can read the name right there on the handles.'

'Where is their Krazy Kar?' said the Chairman.

'What?' said the Head of Drama, weakly.

'Clowns,' said the Chairman, 'have this Krazy Kar, which the doors fall off of, also they get paint poured down their trousers. It goes over very big with kids, which is no small consideration when you handle fifteen per cent of the toy market.'

The Director swivelled suddenly in his seat. There was more white in his eye than heretofore, and the effect of the reflection in it of the twin orange stars was, to say the least, unnerving. Nor was the carefully controlled measure of his voice as reassuring as it ought to have been.

'I have been thinking,' he said, 'and I have decided to open the play with Telly Savalas driving on in a Krazy Kar containing eight Wundatrash Ghosts, across the chest of each of which is advertised some low-price miracle from the Wundatrash range. They have all, of course, come to the wedding, which is to take place in the swimming-pool, downstage right, after which the entire cast will pass among the audience demonstrating the cutlery, crockery and linen to be used at the ensuing breakfast. Every child in the audience will be given a free lollipop and shovel, and the tragedy will close with the happy couple choosing pillowcases. What do you think, BW?'

The Chairman drew on his cigar.

'There's just one thing,' he said. 'Can you get all that into half an hour?'

# I Spy With My Little Eye

*If the latest Finance Bill becomes law, H.M. Inspectors of Taxes will be empowered to 'enlist the co-operation of other members of family' when compiling dossiers on those they suspect of tax evasion.*

Black Hand Esq.,
London Tax Division 67,
St Andrew's House,
Portland Street,
Manchester, M1 3LP

DEAR BLACK HAND ESQ.,                                    29 July 1978

You do not kno me, but I am a frend of Special Agent 196 who sits nex to me in IVb and shoed me his badge in the lav. He also shoed me his Special Tax Strike Force Telescope which folds down into one bit and opens out for stairing at his father which he got off of your offis when he wrote about how his father was selling marroes out of his alotment and not telling you, and a man came down and felt his fathers coller. I also saw the larg lump on his eer where his father lashed out before your man could throe off his disgise and pin him down with this Special Tax Throe And Parralising Grip thàt your Agent 196 says they teach you when you go to this plaice hiden in a forrest and a master of Kung Fu shoes you how to poak your finger through a brik.

Anyway, I do not expect to be one of those agents, not the ones who go around grabing people and bashing there briks up, I realise you have to be fully groan for that, no dout five foot eight also no glasses or denchers simlar to police, but I would very much like to be an agent like 196, I am as big as he is and nine as well, and I would like a Telescope, also the Special Tax

Killer Notebook where you write in what your fathers been up to.

My father is Norman Roy Wibley. He is 36 with thin hare and a small building business, also roofs done and loft conversions, though no glazing. He is almost certnly a crook, he has shifty eyes and is very vilent, often clumping people in the midle of dinner for aciddentally picking there nose and well worth spying on, especially if you had a good Telescope to see him up close and a Secret Tax Pencil With Miracle Rubber On End for writing with.

I am sik of Special Agent 196 going round telling evrybody about how he rescued England from his old man, I think evrybody should have the chanse,

Yours faithfuly,
L. M. Wibley, IVb

DEAR BLACK HAND ESQ.,                              5 July 1978

Thank you for my Telescope and Killer Notebook And Pencil, also the Special Agent Manual on what to look out for, and the badge. Special Agent 196 says he has now got a Junior Tax Commanders Instamatic Camera With Carrying Strapp for leting you know that the Aunt Doreen his father clames as a dependant relative was blone to bits by a Flying Bom in 1944, wel I have got some good stuff too and trust you will not forget this when it comes to sending off cameras, a camera would help no end when caching Public Ennemy Norman Roy Wibley red handed.

Anyway, I am defnitely onto something! Wensday morning after he left in the van, I went into the spair room he uses as his offis, hoping to find evidence of where he was not using said room exclusively for comercial purposes as laid down in my Special Agent Manual, on account of I know he clames it against tax, I have often herd him cakling about how it is the smartest room in the house, new carpets, curtens, real lether armchairs and 'those bugers cannot touch me, it is legitimate offis ferniture, har-har-har, must be six hundred quidsworth of deductibles this year alone, ho-ho-ho, cakle-cakle' etcetera, and I was examining said room for sines of leisure activity such as nude magazines under blotter when I discovered a locked draw in his desk!

Terning imediately to page 32 of my Manual, I folloed the instructions and soon had the draw unlocked. Inside there was a larg black ledger, full of his tinie crimnal writing! Aha, I said to miself, this is A SECOND SET OF BOOKS, as described on pages 14-28! It is here, I said, that he records those cash transactions wich are bringing the country to its nees, and so forth. I will have him, also a Junior Tax Commanders Instamatic Camera and I don't know what else from a graitful Revenue!

I was just about to start reeding this book, when the door opened and the Ennemy himself walked in!

'What have you got there, you little sodd?' he belloed.

I went into a sort of Special Tax Crouch that I thought up miself; I may not be able to poak holes in briks, but I was prepaired to sel my life dearly. Imagine my amazement when he spoted the black book and sudenly went quiet, a strange smile playing about his lipps.

'Oh, I see you have found my old har-har-har, my old diary!' he mutered in a strangled sort of voise, 'I hope you have not read it?'

I shook my hed. He snatched the book from me, and I thought this is it, the clumping will start any minit, but no! Insted, he took out his wollet and gave me a pound noat.

'Let's keep it our litle secret, eh?' he mermered, leeding me to the door.

That was that. I do not kno wear that book is hiden now, but I will find it. Wibley is up to no good, and I will get him!

Yours faithfuly,<br>
197.

DEAR BLACK HAND ESQ.,          8 July 1978

Thank you for the Camera, also the flash cubes. I noat that this means I will be able to photograph black books without waiting for the sunn to come out. I also noat that Special Agent 196 has received a Lone Taxman Repeeting Cap Gun And Consealed Holster just for informing your offis that the three cars in his father's garage are not in fact hired out for weddings and funerals by the Budget Limousine Company, which his father clames to have run at a loss for the last forteen years. I must say, 196 seams to be sitting on a goldmine, I wish Public Ennemy Wibley had a brane like 196's old man.

Stil, my own investigation is coming on very nisely. I have found out that the Ennemy is, as I suspected, Engaged In Other Paid Employment! I have notised that he goes off in the van at least three evenings a week, in his dark blue suit. My mum says it is on account of he is a mason and that he goes off to meet people with their trousers rolled up who hit one another with broom-handels, but you have to forgive her, she is not a Special Agent who has been traned to treet such codswollop with the contemt it deserves. She is not even brite enough to keep her Post Offis Savings Book in a false name like 196's mum, which is why he has got a Magic Luminous Tax Ring and I haven't.

But one thing is sure: Ennemy Wibley is moonliting for undisclosed cash! But I am on to his litle gaim!

Yours faithfuly,
197.

DEAR BLACK HAND ESQ., 11 July 1978

Victory at last! Unlike weedy 196, I have risked life and lim in the jores of death, insted of just sitting in the shedd and writing off noats about how the £2,364.88 my grandfather got last year was not winnings at Wimbledon Dogs but cash rents from Pakistani waiters living in his coal-hole. I don't think it's fair Agents getting Supertax two-wheelers without doing anything brave, just scribling leters.

Not when some of us have been crouching in the back of vans under tarpaulings at ded of nite with the crazed Wibley hertling off on his ilegitimate business!

Anyway, I have got him bang to rites! The van stopped at 24, Omdurman Villas, Edgware, wich is certainly not an adress that appeers on any Wibley tax declaration, and the Ennemy went inside. I wated a few moments, then sliped out of the back of the van and into said house thrugh a downstares window.

All was dark, but I could hear voises from upstares, so adjusting my Personal Tax Mask I have constructed from puting a ballerclaver on bakwards and cluching my Notebook, Pencil, Manual, Telescope and Camera With Flashcube, I crept to the upper flore, lissened, and, crouching like a tigre, pulled open a door!

'AHA!' I cride. 'I have caught you, Norman Roy Wibley, 36! You are making undisclosed cash summs on the side!'

There was much shreeking and shouting at this, and the Ennemy disapeared beneeth the bedclothes. I herd his mufled voise yel:

'I have come here to reed the metre, Albert!'

At this, a larg lady wearing a sheet and standing on the dresing-table cride:

'It is not Albert, it is a blak midgit with a telescope!'

At this, the Ennemy poaked his hed out from the bed, and I imediately took his pitcher! And wile he and his customer were reeling about dazled from the flash, I slamed the door and made my getaway, leeping down the stares with my Special Tax Leep and vanishing into the nite!

I enclose said photograph. You will see that it shoes the Ennemy evading taxes, also the customer in the sheet. Needles to say, the Ennemy has compounded his felny by attemting to bribe me with vast summs and trying to find out if I have other adresses from his black book. He is going about the hous in terror with mad stairing eyes, mutring to himself, and wundring if I have sed anything to my mum about doing things on the side since he has cleerly not disclosed to her this extra summ he is stashing away. I have not; we Agents do not go round telling sivilians.

Only one mistry remanes: what is Wibley doing? He is not reeding a metre as he clamed when grabed. My proffesional opinion is that he is dressmaking, wich is why the customer with the sheet is standing on the dresing-tabel. Either that, or Wibley is a biulder by day and a docter by nite. Anyway, I leeve that to you. I have done my part.

I would like my Supertax two-wheeler in red, but blak would be alrite, too.

Yours faithfuly,
197.

# Die Meistersinger Von Leyland

*The just-opened controversial opera* Bomarzo *is said to have
'brought opera bang into the 1970's, simply because it involves
nudity, sex and violence. But surely there's more to the 'seventies than
that . . .*

## AN OPERA IN THREE ACTS

### CAST

FOSKETTO,
  A Chief Shop Steard
BERYLIA, His Wife
TRACY, Their Daughter
THE DUKE OF LEYLANDO,
  A Management
THE DUCHESS, His Wife
NIGELLO, Their Son
DUDLIO, A Conservative MP
FREDDIO, His Special Friend
GEOFFINI, A Marxist-Leninist
SLIME, An Architect

RATBAGGO,
  His Brother-In-Law
CREEPI, A Journalist
HOWEVER, An Editor
CHUCK, An Anglican Bishop
Chorus of Leyland Workers
Dancing Backbench Poofters,
Japs, Bankers, Heads of
Documentary TV, Addicts,
Bishops, Personalities, Arabs,
Muggers, Spokesmen, Gno-
mes, Social Workers,
Squatters

*ACT ONE, Scene One.*
*Cowley. Before the Chief Shop Steward's Palace. Enter FOSKETTO*

FOSKETTO — What is this, here on the floor? Is it a letter?

CHORUS — It is a bleeding letter. Would you bleeding credit it?

| | |
|---|---|
| FOSKETTO | Would you bleeding credit it? A letter, here on the floor, big as you please! |
| CHORUS | Big as you bleeding please, a letter! |
| FOSKETTO | I shall open it. Look, I have opened it! |
| CHORUS | Stone me, he has only gone and bleeding opened it! |
| FOSKETTO | My darling beloved Nigello, it says here, my heart burns for you like nobody's business. I cannot wait until our two bodies join as one and make wonderful music up the allotments. |
| CHORUS | Up the allotments! |
| FOSKETTO | That's what it says, up the allotments. I shall go on! |
| CHORUS | Stone me, he's going on! |
| FOSKETTO | It is signed—(*turns page*)—AAAAAAGH! (*Staggers*) |
| CHORUS | Bloody hell, he has had one of his turns! |
| FOSKETTO | Gawd almighty, it's one of my turns! |
| CHORUS | It's one of his turns all right, and no mistake! |
| FOSKETTO | Yes, it's definitely one of my turns! Werl, can you blame me? |
| CHORUS | Werl, can you blame him? It must be the bleeding signature what's brought it on! |
| FOSKETTO | Dead right, it's the bleeding signature what's brought it on! |
| CHORUS | Who can it be? Who can it be? |

| | |
|---|---|
| FOSKETTO | Only Tracy, that's all! |
| CHORUS | Not the lovely Tracy, apple of your wossname? |
| FOSKETTO | Yes, the lovely Tracy, my only daughter, only seventeen years old and already a shop steward up the fitting shop, and here's this bloody Nigello having a nibble of her up the allotments! And do you know who this Nigello is when he's at home? |
| CHORUS | No, who is this Nigello when he's at home? |
| FOSKETTO | He is only the bleeding son and heir of the Duke of Leylando, that's who! |

(*Chorus of workers falls on that day's half-finished Mini and smashes it*)

*Scene Two*
*Cowley. The snug of the Plum & Ferret.*
*Enter BERYLIA and DUDLIO.*

| | |
|---|---|
| DUDLIO | My dear Mrs Fosketto, what is your poison? |
| BERYLIA | My poison? Lor lumme, sir, you are not half a caution! I think I shall bust a stay if you do not cease your jesting! |
| DUDLIO | She says she will bust a stay! But she does not mean it, it is just her colourful way of expressing herself. O, how rich is the language of our working classes, how I admire their earthiness and candid wit! |
| BERYLIA | O what charmers you nobs are, sir! Thank you very much, mine is a Campari and Babycham with one of them little wax cherries in it! |

139

| | |
|---|---|
| DUDLIO | With a wax cherry it shall be, and what about a sprig of mint? |
| BERYLIA | Corblimey, sir, a sprig of mint, you certainly know how to treat a lady, also smelling of Brut like a bleeding film star, my head will fair turn any minute! |
| DUDLIO | But to our business, lovely Berylia! As you know, my heart burns for your lovely Tracy, and I wish for her hand in marriage! |
| BERYLIA | In marriage! |
| DUDLIO | In marriage! |
| BERYLIA | And here was me thinking when I saw you grabbing her bust during the excuse-me foxtrot up the works dance you was only after a bit of the other! |
| DUDLIO | The other? Nothing was further from my mind! I wish to join with her in holy matrimony, I can promise her ensuite bathrooms and her own Renault, also a fox stole and two holidays per annum, one guaranteed abroad, and do not forget, dearest Berylia, there will be something in it for yourself! |
| BERYLIA | Something for myself! (*Aside*) Strike me, whatever can he mean? |
| DUDLIO | Hobnobbing with the upper crust is what I mean, such as tea in the House of Commons and possibly a Royal garden party, I shouldn't wonder! |

| BERYLIA | A Royal garden party! I could wear me bottle-green with the crêpe-de-chine collar! I wouldn't have to be bleeding working-class no more! Oh never fear, dear Dudlio, I shall see to it young Trace jumps the right way when you pop the question, she is a loving daughter and not too old for a clip round the ear, neither! |
|---|---|
| DUDLIO | But what of your husband? What of Fosketto? How will he feel about having a Conservative for a son-in-law? |
| BERYLIA | He will welcome it, or I will know the bleeding reason why! Fosketto would not like to have his jollies cut off at source, of that you may be certain. He may go to bed in his cap, but that does not mean he is past it! |
| DUDLIO | Oh, that is wonderful news! I cannot wait to plight my troth! |
| BERYLIA | Well don't hang about, is what I say, we are not getting any younger none of us! |

*(Exeunt)*

ACT TWO, Scene One.
*Westminster. A wine-bar. Enter DUDLIO, SLIME and RATBAGGO, severally.*

| SLIME | But are you sure you can swing it? |
|---|---|
| RATBAGGO | Yes, can you swing it? |
| DUDLIO | You mean, can I swing it? |
| SLIME & RATBAGGO | Yes, can you swing it, can you get a cabinet post, son, we are |

141

not laying out good money on some tuppeny-ha'penny sodding backbench charlie!

DUDLIO  Gentlemen, you have my assurances! As soon as I wed the daughter of Fosketto, I shall be seen as the compromise centrist candidate the country has been waiting for! I shall be the middle-class chap with the common touch! In five years or less I shall be Prime Minister, and we all know what that means.

SLIME  It means eighteen municipal swimming pools, four motorways, thirty-one jerrybuilt comprehensives and eleven town halls, or the boys'll be coming round and they will not be dropping in to pass the time of bleeding day, neither!

DUDLIO  Never fear, gentlemen, the contracts are as good as yours, all I require is a token of your goodwill.

RATBAGGO  A token of our goodwill?

SLIME  He means five hundred large ones in used notes only.

RATBAGGO  Fifty grand in bloody oncers? Pull this one, it has got bells on!

DUDLIO  You cannot buy a double-fronted Tudor residence with two bathrooms plus heated greenhouse for less, and I must cut a bit of a dash with these revolting Foskettos if I am to wed the abominable

|  | Tracy! After all, my old man was a fishmonger and I do not have two pee to rub together, contrary to appearances! |
| RATBAGGO | Fifty grand, if inflation goes on like this, it could knock the bottom out of being bent, shall I give him the envelope? |
| SLIME | Yes, give him the envelope! |
| DUDLIO | Yes, give me the envelope! |
| | (*They give him the envelope. Exeunt*) |

### Scene Two

*Cowley. Up the allotments. Enter TRACY and NIGELLO.*

| NIGELLO | Haw! Haw! Haw! Wasn't that toppin'? |
| TRACY | It was bleeding toppin' all right, no question! |
| NIGELLO | Was it toppin' for you, too? |
| TRACY | Oh, not half, strike me blind if it wasn't toppin' for me, too! |
| NIGELLO | I love you, haw! haw! haw! |
| TRACY (*aside*) | Oh, how my heart breaks when he goes haw! haw! haw! How shall I tell him? (*Weeps*) |
| NIGELLO | What is this? Why are you weepin'? No doubt it is the squashed onion in your hair, next time we shall pick a nice spot among the swedes! |
| TRACY | Oh, my Nigello, there will be no next time! |
| NIGELLO | What? What is this you are sayin'? |
| TRACY | I am to wed Dudlio! |
| NIGELLO | Dudlio! |
| TRACY | Yes, Dudlio! |
| CHORUS | Dudlio! |
| NIGELLO | But he wears a ginger toupee and drops his aitches and is |

|  | generally considered to be a wet! |
| TRACY | You are telling me nothing new, baby! He also suffers from discharges in both ears and is known to carry a cheap chromium syringe in the glove compartment of his A35, but what can I do, my family's happiness is at stake! |
| CHORUS | What a little treasure! They broke the mould when they made her, and no mistake! |
| NIGELLO | This cannot be! |
| TRACY | This must be! |
| NIGELLO | Not if I have anythin' to do with it! |

*(Exeunt)*

## Scene Three
### The Garrick Club. Enter NIGELLO and CREEPI.

| NIGELLO | Haw! Haw! Haw! So you know this for a fact? |
| CREEPI | Oh, yes, I know it for a definite fact, I heard it from the friend of someone who knows the brother-in-law of a practically authoritative source! |
| NIGELLO | Haw! Haw! Haw! And this Dudlio habitually frequents the Locarno, Streatham? |
| CREEPI | He habitually frequents the Locarno, Streatham. |
| NIGELLO | In fishnet tights and a low-cut lamé miniskirt? |
| CREEPI | Either that, or a wet-look sari and wedges! |
| NIGELLO | And why have you not published this before in your rippin' gossip column? |

| | |
|---|---|
| CREEPI | I did not realise it was in the public interest, until you pushed that packet of tenners into my raincoat pocket! |
| NIGELLO | Haw! Haw! Haw! |
| CREEPI | Haw! Haw! Haw! I say, do you remember that last Wall Game... |

*(Exeunt)*

ACT THREE. Scene One.
*Cowley. Before the Chief Shop Steward's Palace.*
*Enter FOSKETTO and BERYLIA.*

| | |
|---|---|
| FOSKETTO | After frank and free consultations with my executive... |
| CHORUS | Conducted in a forthright and open spirit of co-operation... |
| FOSKETTO | I think I speak for all of us when I say that... |
| CHORUS | Despite initial misgivings that it was not in the best... |
| FOSKETTO | Interests of the rank and file, we have decided... |
| CHORUS | Subject, of course, to certain qualifications... |
| FOSKETTO | To allow the marriage to go forward, although we add the rider... |
| CHORUS | That in our opinion Dudlio is a timeserving opportunist toe-rag... |
| FOSKETTO | And a lickspittle jackal of the entrepreneurial clique. But it will not do none of us no harm to have the bugger where we want him, i.e. as my son-in-law! |
| CHORUS | I.e., as his son-in-law! Do us no harm at all, right? |

| | |
|---|---|
| FOSKETTO | Right! |
| CHORUS | Right! |
| BERYLIA | I'll go and order the cake, also some of them gypsy violinists, and a few crates of Worthington. |
| FOSKETTO | Worthington bloody nothing, we're having champagne, don't want people to think we're bleeding tight-fisted, you'll find the keys to the union safe under the seat in my Volvo. And as the management has not seen fit to give us the week off in celebration of this happy event, I shall bring the lads out! |
| CHORUS | And about time, too, we been here all bleeding morning! |

*(Exeunt. That morning's Range Rover rolls off the assembly-line and falls to bits)*

### Scene Two

*Oxford. St Frydwine's Church. TRACY and DUDLIO at the altar. To them, enter ALL. The marriage service proceeds with full High Contemporary Anglican panoply, i.e. Leyland Workers Chorus supplemented by Choir Bootboys Rule OK in Oxford United scarves and Dracula face-masks, preliminary epithalamic recital by the Gay All-Party Parliamentary Committee for Dress Reform, and a Battered Wives Protest Ballet sponsored by the Arts Council, followed by a Sacerdotal Quiz under the aegis of the Nicholas Parsons Lockheed Aircraft Fund Ensemble in which every member of the congregation, having chorally answered the question: 'What was Christ's first name?', is given a red plastic sink-tidy. At this point, the BISHOP wheels his motor-bike to the front of the altar, dismounts and sings:*

| | |
|---|---|
| CHUCK | If there's any of you freaks digs, like, an impediment why these two shouldn't hit the, you know, full marriage bit, let it all hang out now! |

146

| | |
|---|---|
| CHORUS | Let it all bleeding hang out! |
| | (*Long silence, and then—*) |
| FREDDIO | What's all this stuff about him and me in the *Daily Thing*? |
| CHORUS | What stuff? What *Daily Thing*? What is this little fruit rabbiting on about? |
| FREDDIO | What I am rabbiting on about is where me and him is sharing a just redecorated love-nest *à deux* in fashionable Fulham! |
| GAY ALL-PARTY COMMITTEE | Ooooh! |
| FREDDIO | And here he is run off and left me! |
| GAY ALL-PARTY COMMITTEE | The wicked mare! |
| FREDDIO | And me gone through a Cordon Bleu course all for nothing! |
| FOSKETTO | My God, my lovely Tracy and this mincing wossname, that's my Chairmanship of the TUC up the spout! |
| CHORUS | That's his Chairmanship of the TUC up the spout! |
| GAY ALL-PARTY COMMITTEE | You're all so *bigoted*! We think we're going to have a nervous breakdown any minute! |
| CHORUS | Shut your bloody contra-tenor faces, we are down to sing the male parts as per our agreement of the eighteenth ultimo! |
| GAY ALL-PARTY COMMITTEE | Ooooh! Language! |
| BERYLIA | What will become of me? I was going to have the flat over the garage, I have already ordered the bleeding burgundy moquette suite, haven't I? |

| | |
|---|---|
| SLIME | What garage? When bleeding Dudlio gets out of this little lot, he'll be lucky to have his ears on, let alone bloody garages! |
| RATBAGGO | Let alone bloody garages! |
| SLIME | Let alone bloody garages! This has set back our scheme to put a glass roof on Doncaster by ten years, at least! Not to mention the Newport Pagnall Opera House and Zoo! |
| CREEPI | What is this I am hearing? Do I smell corruption? |
| HOWEVER | Of course you bloody do, you smarmy nit! However, Slime Amalgamated Holdings are major advertisers, so give us that bloody Biro! |
| FREDDIO | Never mind his bloody Biro! |
| CREEPI | Never mind my bloody Biro? |
| FREDDIO | Never mind your bloody Biro, what about my new range of non-stick ovenware, who's going to pay for that, I should like to know? |
| CHORUS | Dudlio's fainted! |
| GAY ALL-PARTY COMMITTEE | Loosen his waistband! |
| NIGELLO | No, no, let me through, I'm a fiancé! |
| FOSKETTO | Gorblimey, it's that chinless berk from Management! Everybody out! |
| CHORUS | Out! Out! Everybody out! Let us follow the agreed procedures! |
| TRACY | But I love him! |
| NIGELLO | Haw! Haw! Haw! |
| FOSKETTO | Never mind bleeding haw! |

|  |  |
|---|---|
|  | haw! haw! I am not having no gilded butterfly of the oppressive capitalist tyranny having a gobble of my lovely Tracy! |
| GEOFFINI (*aside*) | I must speak! Now is the time! |
| CHORUS | It is the revered editor of *Bobby Bear's Marxist-Leninist Annual*! It is our honoured brother in the ongoing bleeding class-struggle! But what is he mumbling about under his beard? |
| GEOFFINI | What I am mumbling about is that Nigello may be the son of the loathed inbred fox-butchering Leylando family, but that does not stop him from being the beloved Chairman of the Madame Mao Ad Hoc Solidarity Committee for the Cowley Area! |
| CHORUS | Does this mean he is pledged to overthrow the revanchist elements of the fawning Peking right? |
| GEOFFINI | Yes, it means he is pledged to overthrow the revanchist elements of the fawning Peking right! |
| FOSKETTO | Stone me, would you credit it? |
| CHORUS | Stone us, would you credit it? |
| NIGELLO (*embraces Tracy*) | Haw! Haw! Haw! |

(*Horde of Japs, Bankers, Heads of Documentary TV, Addicts, Bishops, Personalities, Arabs, Muggers, Spokesmen, Gnomes, Social Workers, Squatters dance round the happy couple, singing the famed BARMY CHORUS, and exeunt.*)

# Body And Soul

'The smile of Marabel Morgan is the smile of the Total Woman. In London to launch her book The Total Woman, Mrs Morgan runs Total Woman Inc, a marriage enrichment course which she started in America. Thousands of women have now followed her advice. "Call your husband at the office to say: Hurry home, I crave your body," she suggests, adding that she often meets hers at the door freshly bubble-bathed and wearing only babydoll pyjamas and white boots, causing him to drop his briefcase and chase her round the table.'—Evening Standard

IT HAD NOT BEEN the best of mornings for Mr Dennis Belwether.

It rarely was.

In the dark ruin of his lower lumbar regions, a worn disc throbbed evilly, while in his left knee the shredded cartilage tweaked an agonising descant; nor could he be entirely certain that an arch had not fallen inside a shoe that seemed uncharacteristically full of lumps.

At forty-seven, he reflected, there was a limit to the number of times a man could jump off a wardrobe with impunity. His furred tongue went to his upper plate for the hundredth probe that morning, stencilling the expensive crack: how could he tell his dentist that he had done it when, as he sprinted from the shower, the spike on his *Pickelhauber* had struck the bedroom lintel with a judder that had set his wife's bra-bells jangling fifteen feet away?

He took off his glasses, their ear-pieces still bent from incautious passion, and stared at the thick blue folder labelled Phillimore Holdings which had lain on his desk for three days now, awaiting his deliberations, while the fox-faced executives over at Phillimore paced the Wilton and snapped their pencils and shrieked down the telephone at his boss.

Who had been, Belwether said to himself, remarkably reasonable. Coming into Belwether's office the previous afternoon and finding his employee's wispy head flat on the Phillimore file, snoring, Mr Soames had merely shaken Belwether gently from a dream of flat-chested twinsets toasting crumpets and, as Belwether lifted his pale cheek with its serried dents of Phillimore ring-binding to the painful light, said:

'Why not tell me about it, old chap? Is it a woman?'

To which Belwether had merely blinked wretchedly, a blink being the gesture that occupies the neutral ground between nod and shake; for it *was* a woman, and then again, it wasn't.

But how could one explain that?

'You don't want to chuck away a quarter-century of exemplary double-entry on some bit of teenage stuff from the typing-pool, old chap,' continued Mr Soames, not unkindly. 'There'll be an eight-day chiming bracket clock waiting for you in 1995, you know. Would you jeopardise that for the fleeting joy of how's-your-father?'

He had, it seemed to Belwether, almost patted his shoulder before leaving. The thought filled him with gloomy guilt, again, as he remembered. Mr Soames had offered himself as confidant and priest, almost a friend, just short of a father, and he, Belwether, had merely blinked, rejecting the offered ear, leaving himself adrift and comfortless. All over the world, men were this very moment sitting down together at quiet tables in a thousand bars, to share anaesthetising drinks and friendly bags of cheesy things while each told the other of his sexual peccadilloes and disillusionments, of the wives who hadn't been feeling well lately and the nymphets ravenous for an experienced touch.

But to whom could Belwether go, and with what? What friendship, indeed, even if he had the time to form one, could withstand such ridicule?

He opened the Phillimore file for the twentieth time, and fought to focus his tired eyes on the reeling columns. He reached for his calculator. He unscrewed his pens, one green, one red, one black. The telephone rang.

'It's your wife,' said his secretary, and flipped the switch.

'How many times have I told you,' hissed Belwether into the mouthpiece, 'never to ring me at the office?'

'I crave your body,' murmured Felicity Belwether.

'There's a meeting,' cried Belwether, 'at half-past . . .'

'Passion,' groaned Felicity Belwether, 'billows through me like waves rolling towards the beach, hungry to dash themselves against the rocks. I am lying here clad only in a peep-hole bra and waders, my Dennis!'

'You may not appreciate it, Felicity, but Mr Cattermole of Phillimore Holdings, one of the foremost . . .'

'I have put your long sideburns out ready, my darling,' breathed his wife, 'and your busby has just come back from the cleaners. It will be the matter of a moment for you to jump into your clogs.'

'Oh, God,' muttered Belwether. He put down the receiver. He closed the Phillimore folder. He put the top back on his pens.

The typing pool watched him slink out, limping alternately as he favoured disc and knee.

'Tell Mr Soames I have to see a client,' he murmured automatically, as the door sighed shut behind him.

'*His* age,' said a secretary, studding a cat's eye deftly into her leather bolero, 'bleeding obscene.'

On the Xerox machine, the girl running off eight hundred copies of a Starsky and Hutch poster paused briefly.

'He's probably off up the Jacey,' she said. 'They got *Chinese Emmanuelle in Chains* and *Suburban Tongue*. All he's fit for.'

'Seen his eyes?' enquired a telephonist, breaking off her conversation to her Melbourne boy-friend. 'Don't half stand out. All them little veins.'

'They go like that,' said the tea-girl, adroitly slipping a two-pound jar of Nescafé into her Fiorucci hold-all. 'It's a side-effect. I seen about it in the *Sun*.'

'Serves him bleeding right,' said the secretary. '*His* age.'

On the drizzled street, Dennis Belwether waited for a Number Eleven. It being only noon, none came. He stared into the buslessness, feeling the rain go down under his collar and the wind go up his trousers. He was starting a cold, of that there was little doubt. It would turn bronchial, the way it invariably did, but who would distil the Friar's Balsam, who pour out the

Medinite, who tuck him in and tiptoe about the premises, bearing succulent trays of this and that, silencing children? The last time he had had 'flu, Felicity, driven near-insensate by his presence in the daytime bed, had insisted upon hurling herself on him with merciless regularity, in a variety of foreign uniforms, an activity which, in his enfeebled state, he had been powerless to discourage.

Nor had he ever been able to explain to his two children why, on their return from school, their mother was to be found blacked up and with a feather in her ginger wig, running round the house dressed only in the battle blouse of an Israeli paratrooper.

It would be even worse this time, with his back trouble on top of everything else. She had already shown signs of inordinate interest in the possibility of home traction, and there had been many a lip-smacking suggestion that such games as Nurse And Orthopaedic Patient might soon sneak into Felicity Belwether's illimitable repertoire.

As he stood there, chilled, with the drizzle hardening to sleet and the only refuge from it the voracious premises of 14, Acacia Crescent, old longings stirred within the ravaged frame of Dennis Belwether. They had been stirring more and more regularly in recent months, and he entertained them with less and less shame: he had only one life, he would argue, and had he not passed forty-seven years of it as a faithful husband, and was that not better than par for the course? Was he to go to the long pine box having known only one woman? Was he, too, not as entitled to the free expression of his romantic imagination as Felicity, and could he be blamed if he sought that expression elsewhere than at 14, Acacia Crescent?

Not for the first time, his fingers trembled over the scribbled page at the back of his pocket diary. A blob of sleet fell on it, but fortunately did not disturb the inky number dictated so long ago by Mr Brill of Small Accounts, who had once, in a unique unguarded moment, revealed to him that Mrs Brill had a habit of springing out of cupboards at him, dressed in nothing but angora mittens, which had precipitated Mr Brill's early retirement.

Dennis Belwether looked again at Brill's legacy.

There was a telephone booth across the road.

I will give the bus until I count to fifty, he said to himself.

It did not come. He crossed the road, dialled without thinking, pressed in his hot coin.

When he rang the bell, two flights up above a Greek Street massage parlour, the door was answered by a middle-aged woman in a beige cardigan, grey lisle stockings, worn felt slippers, heavy tweed skirt, and a hairnet.

'Miss Desiree La Biche?' he enquired nervously. 'I rang earlier. Dennis.'

She looked at him over her bifocals.

'I suppose you didn't remember to bring the sprouts?' she said.

'Sprouts?' he said.

'You'll forget your own head one of thee days, Dennis,' she said. 'Come in, don't stand there dripping, I just done that step.'

He went inside. The little corridor smelt of boiled cabbage and Johnson's Pride; a black-and-white dog came up and licked his hand.

'We'll have to take him down and get him wormed,' said Desiree La Biche, 'one of these days. You're always promising.'

'There's never the time,' he replied automatically, following her into a small living-room and sitting down in front of the television set.

'Ten pounds,' said Desiree La Biche.

He sprang up, fumbled for the notes.

'Sorry.' he said, 'almost forgot, ha-ha-ha!'

She put the money on the mantelpiece, under the clock.

'Price of things these days,' she said, 'I was only saying to Mrs Thing this morning, Dennis and me are going to have to give up meat altogether, I said. I know what you mean, she said, I just paid a pound for twelve ounces of ox liver. What? I said, a *pound*, I said. Without a word of a lie. she said. What do you think of that, Dennis?'

'Er, remarkable,' replied Belwether, sitting down again.

'Remarkable, remarkable. that's all you ever say, just so long as you've got your television, personally I don't know what you see in it, lot of rubbish, sit there stuck in front of it, never take me out no more, I was only saying yesterday down the launderette to Mrs, oh, you know, big woman, funny ears, got a son Norman in the navy, no, I tell a lie, army, anyway, what I said was . . .'

As Desiree La Biche droned on, Dennis Belwether felt a delightful numbness seep into his tired limbs, felt the monotonous voice grow distant, felt the evening paper she had put in his lap slip to the floor. He eased his feet from his shoes; he unbuttoned his waistcoat; he let his head fall back against the antimacassar, and let his mind, for the precious half-hour it had been allotted, drift away into luxurious nothingness.

# The Unacknowledged Legislators of the World

*The Poetry Society is falling apart. Rows about personalities, about money, about vanishing booze, fights over control and future plans, mass accusations and resignations have all played their part in what one of the poets has described as the war between poetry and bureaucracy: 'I can't remember when we last talked about poetry at a council meeting' he told the* Guardian. *But wasn't it always like that?*

THE MEETING convened at 2.30 pm.

Mr William Wordsworth immediately rose to say, in his own defence, that there was a tree, of many, one, a single field which he had looked upon, both of them spoke of something that was gone; the pansy at his feet did the same tale repeat: whither was fled the visionary gleam? Where was it now, the glory and the dream?

Mr Andrew Marvell said that that was all very well, but it did not justify £28.40 return rail fare to Keswick, plus £14.26 overnight stay at the Come On Inne and £19.70 for a steak dinner for two, plus three bottles of Bulgarian Riesling. There were plenty of trees and fields within walking distance of the Society's premises perfectly capable of raising questions about the disappearance of visionary gleams and similar cod's wallop. Also, he would like to know why the steak dinner was for two people, and did it have anything to do with the pansy at Mr Wordsworth's feet?

Mr Wordsworth replied that he had found love in huts where poor men lie, his daily teachers had been woods and rills, the silence that was in the starry sky, the sleep that was among the lonely hills, and you could not get that kind of thing in Camden

Town. As to the steak dinner, he did not see what business it was of anybody else's who had joined him for it.

Mr Marvell said that had they but world enough and time, this coyness, Wordsworth, were no crime, but some of them weren't bloody paperback millionaires and couldn't muck about all day nattering, also this was taxpayers' money and not intended for filling Wordsworth's poofter shepherd oppos with foreign booze. His, Marvell's, mistresses never required more than a bottle of Mackeson's beforehand and a Vesta curry afterwards, never mind a night at the Come On Inne.

Mr Wordsworth said that if he must know, the gentleman referred to was Samuel Taylor Coleridge, exemplar of an imagination, which, in truth, was but another name for absolute power, and clearest insight, amplitude of mind, and Reason in her most exalted mood.

Mr Marvell asked Mr Wordsworth to pull this one, it had bells on. No offence to the Hon Member S. T. Coleridge, but he had recently seen him with an arm round a Chief Petty Officer outside a mission near Albert Dock.

Mr Coleridge replied that it was an ancient mariner and he had stopped one of three. If the other two were here today, he continued, they would corroborate his story. The sailor had an idea for a poem and was looking for someone to go halves with him. Anyway, he had a long grey beard and a glittering eye and was probably old enough to be his, Coleridge's, mother. Father.

Mr John Milton rose to enquire about the sailor's idea: did it have anything to do with Man's first disobedience, and the fruit of that forbidden tree whose mortal taste brought death into the world, and all our woe?

Mr Coleridge said no, he thought it was about a gull or something, why did Mr Milton want to know?

Mr Milton replied that he had paid good money for the idea about Man's first disobedience etc. and was buggered if he was going to see it come out in some tatty down-market form, such as rhyming bloody quatrains, before he had had a go at it. He was envisaging something in about twelve books, it could take weeks.

Mr Alexander Pope asked the Council if they intended subsidising Mr Milton's living expenses while he was knocking out twelve books on fruit. No slur intended, he went on, but he had always considered Mr Milton a bookful blockhead, ignorantly read, with loads of learned lumber in his head. Such laboured nothings, in so strange a style, amazed the unlearned, and made the learned smile. Pardon him, he said, but he spoke as he found.

Mr Milton said Mr Pope was a complicated monster, head and tail, scorpion and asp, and Amphisbaena dire, Cerastes horned, Hydrus and Ellops drear.

Mr Thomas Gray rose to say that this was all very well, but it wasn't getting the cracked pan in the Members' Gents repaired, which was why, so he understood it, the meeting had been convened in the first place. Only yesterday, he said, the caretaker had forbade the wade through water to the throne, and shut the gates of mercy on mankind.

Mr John Greenleaf Whittier enquired as to whether the crack was so wide, so deep, that no man living might this fissure weld?

Mr Milton replied that is was a gulf profound as that Serbonian bog betwixt Damiata and Mount Casius old, where armies whole have sunk.

Mr Pope said my God was he really going to go on like this for twelve bleeding books at public expense? Fixed like a plant on his peculiar spot, to draw nutrition, propagate, and rot?

Mr John Keats said that, as convenor of the Plumbing Sub-Committee, he was looking into the whole question of the refurbishment of the toilet facilities. It would not stop at a new pan and lilac seat; what he had in mind was a bower quiet for them, full of sweet dreams, and health, and quiet breathing.

Mr Pope asked Mr Shelley who his friend was.

Mr Shelley replied that he never was attached to that great sect whose doctrine was that each one should select out of the crowd a mistress or a friend, and all the rest, though fair and wise, commend to cold oblivion.

Mr Pope enquired whether Mr Shelley had met Mr Milton. It was his opinion that if they ever put their heads together, they would be able to come up with thirty-eight books on anything. Still, cold oblivion wasn't a bad phrase to describe the Members' Gents, if that was what he was talking about; better than a quiet bower full of people breathing, mind, though he couldn't, of course, answer for Mr Coleridge.

Mr William Shakespeare enquired of Mr Keats why they did pine within and suffer dearth, painting their outward walls so costly gay? Why so large cost, having so short a lease, did they upon their fading mansion spend?

Mr Keats replied that they required an unimaginable lodge for solitary thinkings; such as dodge conception to the very bourne of heaven, then leave the naked brain.

Mr Shakespeare said that if he understood correctly what Mr Keats had in mind, were the walls of the new khazi not going to end up covered in verse jottings, and would this not be an irritation to those wishing to lock themselves in cubicles the better to read the small print on their contracts so as not to end up with three bloody tragedies running simultaneously on Broadway and not even a percentage of the gross after producer's profits?

Mr Keats said he couldn't help it, the stuff just poured out of him. He informed them that he had been taught in Paradise to ease his breast of melodies.

Sir Edmund Spenser reminded them that at the last meeting, he had sought an undertaking that the new lavatory would be painted in goodly colours gloriously arrayed, but had as yet received no word from the committee as to what these colours might be. Three months had now passed.

Replying, Mr Shelley said he rather fancied azure, black, and streaked with gold, fairer than any wakened eyes behold.

Mr Marvell said what about orange bright, like golden lamps in a green night?

Or, interjected Mr Shakespeare, what about having the majestical roof fretted with golden fire? It might cost a bob or two, he added, but it would not half impress publishers.

Mr Gerard Manley Hopkins said that he personally had always rather gone for dappled things.

Green, said Mr Walt Whitman, green, green, green, green, green.

The committee looked at him.

Mr Milton expressed the opinion, after a short silence, that they were not getting anywhere. Chaos umpire sat, he continued, and by decision more embroiled the fray by which he reigned.

Mr Pope asked God to help him.

Mr Wordsworth said that as he had opened the proceedings, it was only fitting, not to say nicely constructed, that he should sum up. He then invited the committee to remember that dust as they were, the immortal spirit grew, like harmony in music; there was a dark inscrutable workmanship that reconciled discordant elements, made them cling together in one Society.

Mr Pope said ho ho ho.

The meeting rose at 4.26 pm.